CROSSING BORDERS

CROSSING

MAX BACA OF LOS TEXMANIACS *with Craig Harris*

Foreword by Daniel Sheehy

My Journey in Music

BORDERS

University of New Mexico Press   Albuquerque

ISBN 978-0-8263-6251-3 (paper)
ISBN 978-0-8263-6252-0 (e-book)

Library of Congress Cataloging-in-Publication data is on file
with the Library of Congress

All photographs in this book are from Max Baca's personal collection.

Cover illustration: [! Designer: Add cover illustration credit/caption info. !]
Designed by Mindy Basinger Hill
Composed in Minion Pro and Resolve Sans

The bajo sexto and the accordion are brothers.

The accordion comes from Texas via the Germans.

The bajo sexto comes from Mexico.

That's why they call it Tex-Mex music.

Acknowledgments   *ix*

Foreword   *Daniel Sheehy*   *xi*

Introduction   *xiii*

ONE   Comenzando (Beginnings)   *1*

TWO   Flaco   *15*

THREE   Creciendo (Growing)   *26*

FOUR   La Música (The Music)   *32*

FIVE   Familia (Family)   *38*

SIX   Cima de Cartel (Headlining)   *46*

SEVEN   Sir Douglas, Augie, and Freddy Fender   *52*

EIGHT   El Origen (The Origin)   *67*

NINE   El Movimiento (Moving)   *72*

TEN   Estirándose (Stretching)   *79*

ELEVEN   Empujando Hacia Adelante
(Pushing Forward)   *84*

TWELVE   Selena   *99*

THIRTEEN   Los Texmaniacs   *102*

FOURTEEN   Grabación (Recording)   *110*

FIFTEEN   Cantando por una Causa
(Singing for a Cause)   *128*

SIXTEEN   Carlos   138

SEVENTEEN   ¿Adónde Vamos desde Aquí?
(Where Do We Go from Here?)   *142*

Epilogue   *149*

Interviews   151

Max Baca's Discography   *153*

Recommended Viewing   *155*

Gringo Lingo   *157*

Notes   *161*

References   *163*

Index   *165*

ACKNOWLEDGMENTS

I want to thank God for the gift of music and the wonderful people he's placed along my journey. To my father and first inspiration, Max D. Baca, Senior: I hope you're proud of me. It's an honor to take your name all over the world. Thank you to my mother, Gloria Baca, the greatest gift God ever gave me.

Thank you, Leonard "Flaco" Jiménez, for taking me under your wing as your right-hand man and bajo sexto player and making me part of your magic, guiding me with your humbleness, teaching me your wise consejos (advice), and being a father to me. Thank you for all the beautiful, priceless memories.

Daniel Sheehy, there are no words to express my gratitude. Thank you for making me part of your familia and patiently guiding me to be the musician I am today. When you said "Los Texmaniacs breathe new life into conjunto music," it made me proud.

Thanks also to my wife (Ping), son (Carlos Baca), grandson (Carlos Max Baca), granddaughter (Mya Jole Baca), brother and musical partner (Jimmy Baca), sisters (Maxine, Renee, Arlene, and Sharlene), grandmother (Millie Lucero), and uncles (Carl and Anthony Lucero). My gratitude goes out to Pat Jasper, Juan Tejeda, Christina Balle, the Guadalupe Cultural Arts Center, Sarah Rucker, Charlie Lockhart, Doug Cox (Vancouver Island Music Festival), Chuck Wentworth (Rhythm & Roots Festival), Barbara Manners (Concert Happenings in Ridgefield, Connecticut), Gilbert Reyes (Hohner), Rock Clouser (H. Jimenez Bajo Sextos), Mingo, Patricia, and the Saldivar family, Pete Reiniger (Smithsonian Folkways), Joe Treviño (Blue Cat Recording

Studios), Julia Olin, Madeline Remez, and all the folks at the National Council for the Traditional Arts (NCTA), Z. and Carol Barbosa (Austin Wholesale), Gilbert Velasquez, Josh Kohn, Jon Lohman, Nick Spitzer, Los Lobos, Milton Walters, Rick Trevino, Ruben Ramos, Joel Guzman, David, Becky and the Farias family, Bobby Fuentes, Rick Fuentes, Chris Rivera, Ray Benson (Asleep at the Wheel), Tara Linda, the Sam Ash Music Company, Ruben and Peggy Castro (Ruben's Place), and my compadres in the Texas Tornados (Augie Meyers, Flaco Jiménez, Freddy Fender, Doug Sahm, and the greatest bajo sexto player, my idol, Óscar Téllez), the Tornado band (Luis Ortega, Ernie Durawa, Speedy Sparks, and the Groove Network), and past and present Los Texmaniacs and their families.

Last but not least, thank you, Craig Harris, for the long hours of interviewing, road trips, and musical gigs that made this book a dream come true. Your soulful vibe and passion for music make it a blessing to be around you. Thank you for your friendship, my brother.

This book is dedicated to everyone passionate about music.

Max Baca

My deepest appreciation is due everyone who graciously shared memories and insights, especially Max Baca, who opened his world to me. Dedicated in loving memory of my mom, dad, corgi, Gene Shay, Paula Ballan, and the pre-pandemic world.

Craig Harris

Max "Donny" Baca is an American original. The music he makes is indistinguishable from the life he has lived, and it could never have happened anywhere else in the world. From the Albuquerque hometown of his youth to the San Antonio hometown of his mature musical years, Max absorbed the music, the culture, and its signature personalities, giving his music its special flavor—just the way New Mexico's Hatch chiles get their own trademark flavor from the nutrients in the soil where they grow. In short, Max doesn't just typify tradition: he is tradition.

He was born into an expansive time for the Texas–Mexican conjunto tradition he personifies. Radio, recordings, television, and migrant agricultural workers took the Rio Grande Valley–born sound far beyond Texan political borders, making it an animating part of life throughout the Northwest, Southwest, Midwest, Florida, and places in between. He was raised at the side of his accordionist namesake father from his earliest years, immersed in a family life filled with good music, food, and spirit, and tempered by the discipline required of the lively, gritty, and demanding nightlife of professional conjunto musicians. Through this intensive and extensive apprenticeship, he learned the fundamentals of the lifestyle, the music, and all four conjunto instruments—accordion, bajo sexto, bass, and drums. He eventually made the weighty, twelve-stringed bajo sexto—what he calls the "grizzly bear of guitars"—his life partner.

As his music-drenched life progressed, Max attached himself to the best mentors the tradition offered. The incomparable accordionist Leonardo "Flaco" Jiménez took Max under his wing. Max idolized Flaco's bajo sexto player, Óscar Téllez, who epitomized the instrument's gold standard of excellence of the time. For recordings from the past, he turned to quintessential bajo sexto pioneer Santiago Almeida, who, together with accordionist Narciso Martínez, set the music's seminal sound. And then he went further afield, accompanying Flaco in the popular country-rock-conjunto fusion group Los Texas Tornados in the 1990s.

The Tornados marked a milestone for Max as he launched a fresh vision for his own music. He grew the traditional conjunto sound, both through his extraordinary musicianship and by adding new ingredients from rock, blues, and country. He enshrined the dual inward- and outward-looking spirit of his creative vision in his new group's name—Los Texmaniacs. With a Grammy Award and additional Grammy nominations to its credit, the group came to be seen as a beacon of fresh, fun-loving, fearlessly creative conjunto music, firmly planted deep in the heart of Texas-Mexican tradition. Half the story of Los Texmaniacs is Max himself; when you mention his name to musicians, they tend to smile and nod knowingly, their memories lovingly filled with the foibles of "Max stories." He has all the traits of an extraordinary artist—a dreamer and a respected musician's musician, deeply engrossed in his music and running on "Max time" rather than that dictated by the everyday demands that shape most people's lives. Max is uncommonly special and much beloved. I am proud to call him my friend.

This book's story, captured by its author, Craig Harris, is more than a story of Max Baca: it's a deeply personal window into a vital slice of American culture. As Americans, it's our story, too, and it's a great read. Welcome to Max's world—our world.

Daniel Sheehy, PhD
CURATOR EMERITUS,
SMITHSONIAN FOLKWAYS RECORDINGS

(Craig Harris)

This book is the product of hours of interviewing and research. The recollections of Max Baca, pace-setting bajo sexto player, leader of the Grammy-winning Los Texmaniacs, and longtime Flaco Jiménez accompanist, are fleshed out by observations from his mother (Gloria Lucero Baca), brother and former bandmate Jimmy, son Carlos, musical compatriots Flaco Jiménez, Augie Meyers, Peter Rowan, and Rick Trevino, members of Los Texmaniacs past (David Farías) and present (Josh Baca, Noel Hernandez, and Lorenzo Martínez), producers Daniel Sheehy, Joe Treviño, and Steve Berlin (Los Lobos), and others.

Max Baca—or Donny, as family and friends call him—has expanded Tex-Mex, conjunto (small band), and Tejano music with the imaginative flourishes of his twelve-string bajo sexto. Descended from seventeenth- and eighteenth-century Spanish stringed instruments including the bandolón, guitarra séptima, and jarana jarocha, the bajo sexto's steel strings are tuned an octave below those of a standard guitar. The last two are tuned up a half step—E, A, D, G, C, F, low to high. The first three pairs are tuned in octaves and the last three in unison. "The bajo sexto is the grizzly bear of guitars," Max explains. "Its strings roar when you play it. It handles the bass and the rhythm, like a bass and a guitar at the same time. It's a percussion instrument too. The strike of the pick sounds like a snare drum. You do it all on one instrument—a bajo sexto. But a bajo sexto isn't a guitar. You can only bend a bajo sexto string so much. You have to slur the strings to get them to sound the way that you want them. Other bajo sexto players don't try for a screaming guitar-like sound. They stick to basic riffs, keeping it simple. But I

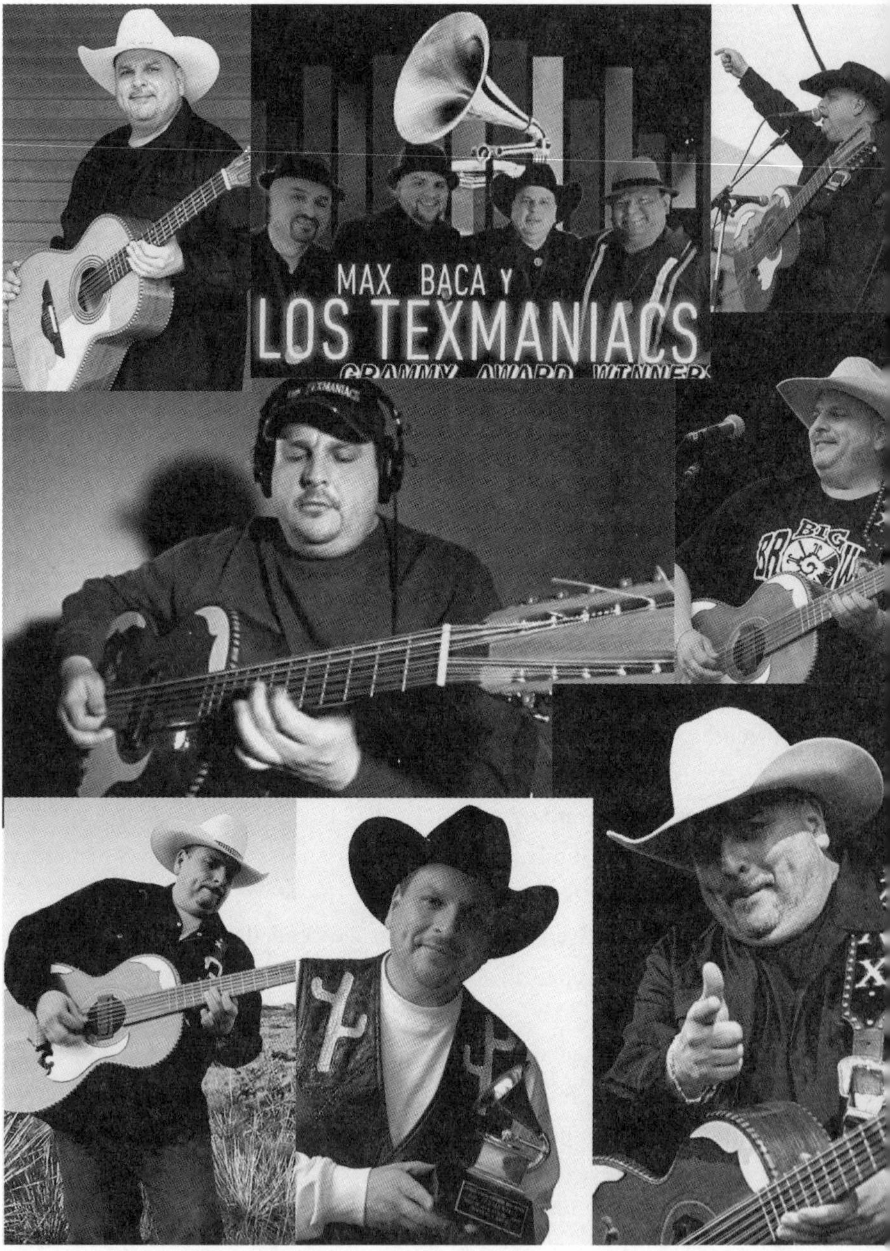

Max Baca y Los Texmaniacs collage

Hard Rock Café, Albuquerque, New Mexico

asked myself, 'Why can't I play that B. B. King, Eric Clapton, or Jimi Hendrix riff on bajo sexto?' Even though I have a traditional instrument and play conjunto, Norteño, and Tex-Mex music, why couldn't I also play the blues and rock & roll I was listening to?"

"The bajo sexto is meant for rhythm," legendary San Antonio–born accordionist Flaco Jiménez (b. 1939) points out, "but Donnie does solos. He knows progressions. He can go from straight polka and conjunto music all the way to rock & roll. He does it by heart, not mechanically. He feels what he plays. Like Carlos Santana, he lets it all out."

"I've always enjoyed Max's sound," says Noel Hernandez, bass player, harmony singer, and arranger for Los Texmaniacs since 2014. "He could plug into the crappiest amp and still have his particular tone. It exemplifies what the bajo sexto is about. He's very dynamic. He could be heavy on it, where it sounds like thunder, and then, when it comes to the traditional stuff, he's the cream of the crop."

The Tejano Music Awards named Max Baca the year's "Best Bajo Sexto Player" nine years in a row. They presented Los Texmaniacs with a couple of "Best Conjunto" awards. Max, however, finds the label "Tejano" misleading. He says, "I don't like to say that we play Tejano music. That's way too big a genre of music. It could be anything played by a Mexican American in Texas, whether it's blues, swing, or rock & roll, or electronica."

According to Eduardo Díaz, director of the Smithsonian Latino Center, "Los Texmaniacs preserve the traditional Tex-Mex sounds, but they're adventurous, not stuck in tradition." Juan Tejeda agrees. He is the accordionist and singer of Conjunto Aztlan and cofounder of the annual Tejano Conjunto Festival. "Los Texmaniacs has it all. They're very much in the tradition of Flaco Jiménez, but they push it over into rock, blues, rhythm & blues, and country music. They throw in Latino rhythms. It's all part of the process. They're always moving forward and learning new things—experimenting. They're the only ones touring and putting conjunto music on the national and even international circuit. They're an exciting band."

Max recalls that when Los Texmaniacs once played in Europe, an emcee announced, "From the United States, here's Los Texmaniacs playing authentic Mexican music, eating tacos, and drinking tequila." "No! No! No! No!" Max responded. "Our ancestors may have been Mexican, Spaniard, or different crossbreeds, but we're Americans, born in the United States."

Being from New Mexico, Max and his nephew, Los Texmaniacs' accordion player Joshua "Josh" Baca (b. 1991) approach music differently than do Tejano musicians. "We're not from Texas," Josh reports, "but representing Texas music and expressing that culture to the world is awesome. Sometimes I'll hear Max playing around the beat—New Mexican/Native American chicken scratch style—then, he'll lay back and play hardcore San Antonio down-South conjunto style." Noel Hernandez adds, "It's a different flavor than what we have in South Texas. I never imagined that a kid in New Mexico would be listening to the same music that I did. It came to me that our music is connected by the Rio Grande River. It starts in New Mexico, where Max and Josh are from, and goes to where I'm from in the Rio Grande Valley. Dan Martínez, our drummer, is originally from Laredo, up the river from me."

As Los Hermanos Baca (the Baca Brothers), Max and his older brother Jimmy (Baltazar James Baca, b. 1962) won awards from the Hispanic Music Association in 1985, one for "Conjunto of the Year" and the other for "Vocal Duo of the Year." The brothers would go their own ways, but Max would continue making Tex-Mex history. After winning a "Best Tejano Recording" Grammy for Los Texmaniacs' first Smithsonian Folkways album, *Borders y Bailes* (2010), Max donated an electric bajo sexto to the Hard Rock Casino in Albuquerque. They kept it in a glass case with lights. There was a plaque that read, "Max Baca, the first New Mexican to win a Grammy." "That was an honor," he said. "The state was proud."

Los Texmaniacs' second Smithsonian Folkways album (and sixth overall), *Texas Towns & Tex-Mex Sounds*, received a Latin Grammy nomination in 2012. Their next album, *Cruzando Borders*, was nominated for a Grammy in the "Best Regional Mexican Album" category in 2019.

Rick Trevino, Lyle Lovett, Joe Ely, Rick Fuentes, Alejandro Escoveda, Kevin Fowler, Bobby Flores, Ray Benson (Asleep at the Wheel), and Los Lobos' David Hidalgo, Cesar Rosas, and Rick Berlin have appeared on Los Texmaniacs' albums. The current lineup includes Noel Hernandez on bass, Josh Baca on accordion, and Dan Martínez on drums. "Max is the bandleader," points out Peter Rowan, who toured with the band in 2019 and 2020, "and he's fluent in the ideas the band is expressing. We've talked about being bandleaders and agreed that when you could just relax and let the band do its thing, that's the best. Then you're not the bandleader but part of the music. You can let the whole thing carry you and everybody else. Max is a beacon for the oneness of the band."

Max met Flaco Jiménez, a musician twenty-eight years his senior, when he was just seven years old, and has played alongside him for years. The pair joined Doug Sahm, Augie Meyers, and Freddy Fender in the Tex-Mex supergroup the Texas Tornados, and they played with Freddy, Joe Ely, Ruben Ramos, Rick Trevino, and Los Lobos' Cesar Rosas and David Hidalgo on Los Super Seven's Grammy-winning album in 1998. Flaco and Max also played on a song ("Sweethearts Together") on the Rolling Stones' double-platinum 1994 album *Voodoo Lounge*. Besides the two albums Flaco recorded for Arista, *Flaco Jiménez* (1993) and *Buena Suerte, Señorita* (1996), Max played on *Said and Done* (1998), *Sleepytown* (2000), and *Squeeze Box King* (2003). *Flaco Jiménez* and *Said and Done* won Grammy Awards. In 2014, Smithsonian Folkways released *Flaco and Max—Legends and Legacies*, featuring songs the accordionist and bajo sexto player played with their fathers. They've done another ten albums that Flaco released on his own.

"Max is so deferential to Flaco," observes Daniel Sheehy, the retired Smithsonian Folkways director/producer who signed Los Texmaniacs in 2008. "He loves him so much. He sees him as a second father. As a musician, he's totally engaged with whatever Flaco's doing—right there, glued to him. You feel this sense of warmth. Flaco feels the same way towards Donny. That's what he calls Max."

Max has played on hundreds, if not thousands, of recording sessions at Blue Cat Studio in San Antonio. Owner Joe Treviño reports that "Max is arguably the most recorded bajo sexto player on the planet: rock, blues, and zydeco to conjunto, Tejano, and everything in between. He covers so much ground. He's played on all the important Tejano records, from Ruben Ramos to Little Joe [Hernández] and Dwayne Verhyden. He's on twenty-five Tejano Conjunto Festival records, not only with Los Texmaniacs but also with Flaco, Mingo Saldivar, and so many I can't remember them all."

The following chapters combine Max Baca's own recollections, notes on the instruments and central figures of Tex-Mex music, and observations by Max's bandmates and family. The story is not always a pretty one, but it gives a glimpse into the life of one of the most talented performers of this rhythmic, mesmerizing, thoroughly American music.

CROSSING BORDERS

ONE

COMENZANDO

(Beginnings)

I was born on the twenty-first day of October 1967. There's a photograph of me at four and a half or five. I'm onstage with my dad, sitting on a chair, holding an accordion. We were at the Calderon Ballroom in Phoenix. My dad was an accordion player and the leader of Max Baca y Su Conjunto Norteño. They wore black pants, black boots, white shirts, brown suede vests, cowboy hats, and gun holsters.

A conjunto is a small group or ensemble. Since the 1940s and '50s, the bass, drums, and bajo sexto have driven the groove while the accordion plays the lead. Eduardo Díaz, director of the Smithsonian Latino Center, explains, "The accordion was a foreign instrument in Mexico. It came from the Chinese *sheng*, the ancient mouth organ. Somehow, it evolved in the eastern part of Germany around the mid-1800s."

"Music in the conjunto repertoire isn't Mexican," adds Gilbert Reyes, project developer for the Hohner Instruments Company. "Polkas, redovas, and schottisches came from Europe."

Hohner, the premier accordion manufacturer, "has been around since 1857 making harmonicas," says Reyes, " but they didn't start making accordions until 1903, a year after its founder, former clockmaker Matthias Hohner, passed away. His five sons had wanted to get into the accordion business, but he didn't."

Frederick Veerkamp played a strong role in spreading the instrument's popularity. Reyes says that he came to New York in 1903 "to work in the first office Hohner opened outside of Germany. It opened two years before to distribute harmonicas. Frederick Veerkamp's duty was to sell Hohner products including accordions. He started in New York and traveled through the states, went through Louisiana and Texas, and ended up in Mexico City in 1904. Four years later, he opened the first Hohner distributorship in Mexico City. From 1903 to 1908, there was a flow of product from harmonicas to accordions going from the United States into Mexico and then through the ports of Mexico once they established distribution.

"The harmonica was simple to play and easy to transport. You didn't need amplification. You could pick it up and start playing. The accordion was the same thing. It could handle the bass and treble notes. You didn't need accompaniment to make music. 'Let's have a party!' Take out the accordion and start playing music for dancing. It didn't take much. That's why it became popular."

Reyes says that "a one-row diatonic accordion is like a harmonica. Push or pull, you get a different note. Playing a two-or-three-row piano accordion is like having two or three harmonicas. Mexicans started using three-row accordions and came up with a scale. Instead of going in and out, like with a harmonica, they could just go on the draw or the pull of the bellows and play fast."

Piano accordions were popular until the mid-1950s. According to Reyes, two hundred and fifty thousand of the instruments were made annually for US distribution. "They were that popular. Then what happened? Rock & roll came into the picture—Elvis Presley, the Beatles, and so on. The piano accordion became uncool. Baby boomers were the first to dismiss it. They didn't like their parents' accordion music, but, at the same time, the diatonic accordion was growing in the Latino communities, especially in the US. There were fifty-nine million Latinos in the States as of 2017. They've kept their music alive. Young Latinos listen to their parents' and grandparents' music."

The father of Tex-Mex conjunto music, Narciso Martínez (1911–1992), was born in Reynosa, Tamaulipas, Mexico. He spent most of his life on the other side of the border in La Paloma, Texas, near San Benito. Inspired by the music he heard played by German, Polish, and Czech immigrants, he developed a repertoire of instrumental jigs, polkas, mazurkas, and schottisches that he played on accordion. "The rich people, the high class, liked orchestras with saxophones," Flaco Jiménez explains, "but Narciso Martínez started it all—Tex-Mex and conjunto."

Early Tex-Mex accordionists played under a tree or beside a campfire. Their squeezebox melodies got people to dance, but some kind of accompaniment was needed for musical depth. Conventional guitars had too thin a sound. Martínez tried having a harp do the bass notes, but the harp player struggled to be heard over the accordion.

Meeting Santiago Almeida (1911–1999) in early 1934, Martínez found what he had been seeking. Almeida, a native of Skidmore, Texas, a small town between San Antonio and Corpus Christi, grew up playing with his seven brothers in a family band, La Orquestra Almeida. The group, comprising clarinet, flute, bajo sexto, and string bass, played an extremely wide range of dance music. Almeida had first taken up bajo sexto at the age of fifteen. Martínez found him a monster talent. He took the whole load with his bass picking and strumming, allowing Martínez to abandon the old Germanic two-hand style of accordion playing and focus on the left-hand melody buttons. That meant he could play faster, with more attitude.

Before bands added standup basses, bajo sextos played the low notes. When I got my first Macias bajo sexto, I followed the lead of most modern players who take the top two strings off and just use ten strings, sometimes only eight. Flaco told me that young players use only two strings. When I started playing with him, he asked me, "Donnie, where are your top strings? They're there for a reason." He showed me how to use the bass and treble notes at the same time. It made a difference in the fullness of the sound—the lower register.

Listening to early conjunto records—the 78s—I can hear that the bajo sexto player has such depth, yet he's also got the melody, the rhythm, and the strike. That clank sounds like a hi-hat. When you're playing bajo sexto, you're the bass player, the rhythm guitarist, and the snare drummer. When it's sounding great, that's what intrigues me. Eloy Bernal of El Conjunto Bernal played like that; it brought out the richness of the instrument.

Released in 1935, Narciso Martínez and Santiago Almeida's first single—the polka "La Chicharronera," backed with the schottische "El Tronconal"—on the Bluebird label, became a hit. They continued to lay the foundations of the music until the 1950s, when Almeida moved to Washington state.

Martínez and Almeida stuck to instrumentals, but Clarksdale, Mississippi–born, Kenedy, Texas–raised accordion player/singer Valerio Longoria (1924–2000) sang mariachi songs and poems by Mexican poets. His first canción ranchera, "El Rosalito," released in 1947, became a much-covered classic. The following year, he introduced the modern drum set to conjunto music. Juan Tejeda calls Longoria's hall-marks "a smooth accordion style with long extended runs."

The first time I came on stage, my father's band was taking a break. "All of a sudden, we heard the accordion playing," my mom remembers. "I looked up and there's Donny with his dad's accordion, playing and playing and playing."

My dad's bass player came onstage first. Then, as my mom recalls, "Donny's dad came on stage and strapped the accordion to his shoulders."

Max Don Baca

I started a song and stopped in the middle. My dad looked at me. I asked him, "Do you want me to play the second half?" "Play the whole thing!" The rest of the band jumped in and backed me up.

People started running up to the stage, throwing pennies, nickels, quarters, and dollars. I thought to myself, "I'm rich!" I was in heaven, thinking about all the Bazooka bubble gum and candy I was going to buy.

I was named after my dad, Max Don (Macedonio) Baca. He was born on April 19, 1924 and spent most of his life in Albuquerque. A veteran of World War II, he had been an infantryman stationed on the front line in Germany and Belgium, one of those guys who ran off the rafts shooting. He never liked talking about it, but he told my brother and me stories. We'd go deer hunting and sit under a tree. A plane would fly over and he'd say, "I remember when I was in the war . . ."

He told us that he could tell the difference between American tanks and German tanks just by hearing them. German tanks sounded brutal and very loud. When they came over the horizon, the ground shook. He remembered the men being given shovels and digging holes, as quickly as you could imagine, to get out of harm's way.

After he got home, he had nightmares. My brother Jimmy, sister Maxine, and I would wake in the middle of the night and hear him screaming. He had been a prisoner of war and was missing for the longest time, about three years. They had him working at a concentration camp as a cook. Toward the end of the war, friends of his were being punished and they weren't given anything to eat. When it came time to go back to his quarters, after work, he put rice in his boots to share with his friends.

My dad grew up poor. As a child, he worked in the fields with his dad, my grandfather, Baltazar Baca. He was Apache. I never met him. We have land—twenty acres—that he passed down to us. It's in a mountainous area. He died the year I was born. He received a purple heart in World War I. I have his medal.

My dad was a youngster when he went away to war. When he came home, he brought an accordion. It was more like an Irish accordion, the kind used for playing jigs and reels. My grandfather had an old button accordion and my dad, from time to time, would pick it up and play. He was self-taught. He was so attracted to Narciso Martínez's kind of music that he'd go to Juárez, Mexico, about four and a half hours from Albuquerque, to hear Norteño bands. They played Mexican and Spanish music with the drive of military brass bands. He liked the sound of an accordion and saxophone and learned to play in that style.

When I was born, my dad owned a nightclub, the Bondman's Lounge, in downtown Albuquerque. He worked as an accountant and bail bondsman, but he played music almost every night— Monday through Saturday. He'd pack them in; there was always a full house. "There would be as many people on a Monday night as there were on Saturday," my brother Jimmy remembers. "My dad's band was actually a quintet. They had two accordion players." On Sundays, my dad hired a local group, Manny and the Casanovas, to play. Uncle Toño played drums. Jimmy remembers them as "an orchestra with brass, saxophones, and trumpets."

My dad made sure there was popcorn

Pfc. Macedonio Baca Missing in Action

Pfc. Macedonio Baca, son of Mr. and Mrs. Baltazar Baca, 133 River View Road, has been reported missing in action over Germany since Nov. 27. Pfc. Baca was overseas seven months with an infantry division and has been in the service 15 months. Pfc. Baca has five sisters, they are Domitilia Garcia, and Sirilia, Ermelinda, Margaret, and Rosalie Baca all of Albuquerque. A brother-in-law, Sgt. Felizardo Garcia, is serving with the Seventh Cavalry in the Philippines. Sgt. Garcia and

M. Baca

Max Don Baca was a prisoner of war for three years

or peanuts on all the tables—something salty—so people would drink. He was a smart businessman. Before the war, he'd go up into the mountains with a chainsaw, chop down trees, and sell a truckload of firewood. Jimmy says, "After selling wood all day, he'd go out and play a gig at his nightclub, a house party, or a hall someone rented for a wedding." My mother remembers, "My husband always had a business, but he loved to play accordion. He didn't make a living playing music, but it helped."

A year or two after I was born, my dad sold the nightclub—it's now the Bank of New Mexico—and started investing in property. He quit the bondsman position because it got to be too dangerous. He had to pick up guys who skipped bail and hadn't paid him. He became an accountant and opened Max Baca's Income Tax Service, but he also started taking music more seriously and recorded his first album, *Vamos Albuquerque!* (*Let's Go Albuquerque*). He composed the title polka. The LP's liner notes, written by Senator Pete Domenici, talked about how Albuquerque was growing.

My dad played a role in introducing chicken scratch music, or waila, to the Natives in Tucson, Phoenix, and Winslow, Arizona, and western New Mexico. Waila is Norteño music without the singing. Many Yaquis, Aztecs, Mayans, and Tohono O'odham spoke Spanish, but they were embarrassed to sing. It was all instrumental music.

When she was young, my mom worked at an A & W restaurant. That's where my dad met her. He already had children, three daughters from a previous marriage. Then we came along—my brother, younger sister Maxine, and me.

My dad's daughters—my stepsisters Renee, Arlene, and Sharlene—lived with us. Their mother passed away at an early age and my mom raised them. Sharlene is a flight attendant for United Airlines, the head attendant on overseas flights.

Renee told me she knew I loved music because, when she was pregnant with her first child, she'd pick me up, put me on top of her belly, and dance. When she stopped, I'd kick my feet and say, "C'mon, giddy up." She danced to put me to sleep; I was so full of energy. The last thing I wanted to do was go to bed.

A native of Albuquerque, my mother was the oldest of four daughters. She had three sisters and two brothers. My grandmother, Millie Lucero, raised them. My grandfather left her with all the kids and moved on. He remarried and started another family. My grandmother never did. She's ninety-six years old. We're blessed to still have her. We talk from time to time. Her mind is still as sharp as a tack; she's a strong woman.

My mother's father, Patricio or "Pat," passed on a while back. I remember him visiting when I was young. He'd come in my room, close the door, and say, "Let me see your guitar, boy." He never played music professionally, but he was a big Ernest Tubb fan. He'd grab the guitar and start singing "Waltz Across Texas." Then he'd take me to get ice cream or to a movie.

Gloria and Max Don Baca Sr.
(Max's parents)

I got to see him right before he passed away. He had cancer, but he was home. I drove from Texas, where I was living, to Albuquerque to see him. He sat up when I got there, looked at Uncle Carl, and said, "That boy can play that guitar." I visited with him and told him that I loved him. He said, "Don't worry, I'll be fine. We'll play music together." That was the last time I saw him.

My mom grew up with her mother, brothers, and sisters in an old house without a bathroom. They used an outhouse. She was very appreciative of everything she had. When she was a kid, she and her siblings got a new pair of shoes once a year. We'd get a new pair when we needed them. My mom would complain that our feet were smelly and take us to buy new shoes.

My dad was extremely strict. It was always "Yes, sir" and "No, sir." If you sat down at the dinner table wearing your ballcap, he'd knock it right off your head. He demanded respect, but he was a provider. He did whatever it took so we wouldn't suffer. We always had a roof over our heads. We didn't live a hard life. We never starved. My dad would come home and ask if we'd eaten.

My mom's cooking was always the best. Oh my, was it good. She cooked every day, making beans, handmade tortillas, or sopapilla (fry bread) with so much love. It was as though she was thinking of each of us while she cooked. She put tender love and care into food.

Of course, we had flame-roasted Hatch green chiles. They're only grown in Hatch, New Mexico. They're different than a jalapeño or habanero pepper, really tasty. If you go to a McDonald's in New Mexico, you can order a quarter-pounder with green chile; they're so good.

After harvesting the crop in October, the workers would rotate the chiles on a wire-mesh cylinder over a fire. My mom would bring home a gunnysack full. They smelled so good. The whole family would get together to peel the chiles, getting the stems and the seeds out. We'd put the chiles into a food processor and chop them up and have green chile (chile verde) with hamburgers or in soup. Beans, squash, corn, and chile, there was always some kind of heat. You'd burn your mouth. It's part of the culture.

Whenever the Texas Tornados and I played in New Mexico, we'd stop at my mom's and she'd cook for us. Sometimes Doug Sahm followed in his car; he loved to drive. We once played in Santa Fe and had a show in Albuquerque the following night. We went to eat at my mom's. Freddy Fender was diabetic and he couldn't eat a lot of things. The first time he visited, he told my mother, "I came, Mrs. Baca, because I've heard so much about your enchiladas." Before we ate, Freddy asked, "Mrs. Baca, is that your blue Riviera car outside?" My mom said, "Yeah, but it's broke." It had been parked there for more than three months. She had changed the battery and the alternator, but couldn't get it to start. Freddy said, "Let me take a look at it."

While everybody else was eating, Freddy disappeared. It was getting time to leave for the gig, and no one had seen him for a while. Where's Freddy? Lo and behold, he was on his back, underneath my mom's car. He had tools and was doing something. You could see his boots. He was wearing his outfit for the gig, but he was on the floor like a mechanic. When he crawled out, dirt covered his entire back. We dusted him off. Then he said, "Okay, Mrs. Baca, try to start it." Sure enough, the car started. I don't know what he did, but it worked.

Even when he wasn't touring with the Texas Tornados, Doug would stop at my mom's whenever he drove through New Mexico. He'd call a day before. She'd make green chile chicken enchiladas. He called her enchiladas the "key to the West." My mother remembers: "Doug would call and say, 'Mrs. Baca, I'm just checking to see if you're going to be home. I'd like to stop and say hello.' I'd say, 'Sure Doug, I'll be here.' I'd run to the store and get all the ingredients."[1]

One time, Doug called, and my mom made a green chile casserole. For some reason, Doug didn't show until two days later. He started knocking on the door. My mom answered and said, "You were supposed to come yesterday." He explained that something had happened and apologized for not getting there sooner. She said, "Come on in. Everyone came last night and ate the casserole, but I have a little left." She warmed it for him and said, "Here you go—a little is better than nada." Doug stopped what he was doing and said, "Wait a minute, Mrs. Baca, give me a pencil or a pen and a napkin, there's a song here."

Sure enough, he wrote a freaking song right there in my mom's kitchen—"a little is better than nada / sometimes you want the whole enchilada." It became a hit. They used it in the movie *Tin Cup* with Kevin Costner and Rene Russo. We performed it during the Hollywood premiere. We played at a private VIP party for the actors, director, and crew of the movie on the roof of a hotel.

Growing up, we'd sit down for dinner as a family. We weren't allowed to take our plates and run off to our rooms to watch television. We had to eat with everyone. That was important to my mom and dad.

Music was also important. My mom had a collection of hardcore conjunto albums. I remember this big stereo that looked like a big wooden dresser. You lifted the top and there was the turntable. It had cabinets underneath it, where she kept albums. It wasn't very loud, but it had a clear sound. We'd listen to it while eating dinner. Sometimes, when she was cooking, my mom would listen to it and dance in the kitchen. She'd have her apron on, waving a spatula. She loved music; she just didn't want to see her kids struggle.

When my dad listened to the radio, it was always Spanish or Mexican music, conjunto music. On our own time, we'd go into our room and listen to whatever we wanted. Both of my mother's brothers were drummers. The younger of the two, Anthony, played drums for a short time for my dad. He was a good drummer. I learned a lot from him. We call him "Toño." He helped my dad at the bar.

I love both uncles, but Uncle Carl is something else. When I was growing up, he'd say, "Someday, I'm going to be your personal manager." He played drums for my brother and me for a while, but he was a heavy drinker. He was a veteran of the Vietnam War. After he got home, he started drinking—a lot. By the time we'd start a gig, he would have already downed a half pint of whiskey. The first drummer that walked into the club he'd give his sticks and say, "Sit in." Then he'd go to the bar and drink some more.

Thank God, he's sober, for more than thirty years. He still visits me for two weeks every other month. He has a room in my house. He calls me, or I call him, and he gives me advice. He's never judged me. He tells it like it is and he speaks nothing but the truth. He doesn't sugarcoat anything. He's straight up. When it comes to music, he says, "There are musicians and there are instrument owners. I have a credit card. I can buy a saxophone or a drum set, but can I play them? No!"

My dad was my grandparents' only son, but he had five sisters. When he played the accordion, they'd dance. He mostly played polkas, but he had a unique way of playing them, sort of a mix of German and Native American. He recorded seven albums, lots of 45s, and some 78s. He even recorded some eight-track tapes.

My brother and I picked up my dad's accordion before we knew what we were doing with it. Jimmy started playing when he was twelve. I followed quickly. After we got home from school, we had to each practice the accordion for thirty minutes. There was only one accordion for Jimmy and me, so we'd run home to be the first to practice. Jimmy was more interested in the accordion; he usually beat me home.

"As soon as we'd get home," Jimmy remembers, "we'd jump out of the car and haul butt to get to the accordion first. We had to be the first to give it a slap. If I got it first, I could practice as long as I wanted, sometimes until dark. That accordion, we put it through some hard times. We played the hell out of it."

"I remember them pleading to let them play first," recalls my mother. "'It's my turn.' I'd say, 'Okay, you play for X amount of time and then give it to him.' It seemed like Donnie always won."

I remember practicing the accordion, looking out the window, and seeing my friends playing or riding their bikes.

The first two songs I learned—"The Monterrey Polka" and "In the Mood"—were taught to me by my dad. The first had been the B side of a single by Fannin County, Texas' Bill Boyd & His Cowboy Ramblers in 1948, and the second had been a big-band hit for Glenn Miller in 1939.

My dad took me to a pawn shop when I was eight or nine and asked, "Do you like this bass guitar?" I didn't know anything about the bass, but he said, "I'm going to buy it. You have one week to learn it. We have three gigs next weekend and we need a bass player." I had no choice. In a week, I learned

Childhood memories

to play the bass. Nobody taught me. I watched my dad's bass player and saw how he held his bass. I had been playing accordion, knew a little about the guitar, and was familiar with the songs. It came relatively easily. I put an album on the record player, listened to it, and thought, "Okay, it sounds like this."

"Early conjuntos would get just about anybody to play bass," Noel Hernandez explains. "Tuning was an issue, but the energy was there. The bass plays in unison with the bajo sexto on the downbeat of a polka. It creates space for the accordion and bajo sexto. Sustaining a note creates harmonic texture. Sometimes, it comes naturally. You don't have to think about it; it just happens."

I wouldn't say that my first day went perfectly but I got through it. I remember going with my dad and brother to American Indian reservations and playing. There were periods when I wanted to quit but we were playing music to survive. It was our way of bringing food to the table. We played at weddings and quinceañeras celebrating a girl's fifteenth birthday. On Fridays and Saturdays, we played in nightclubs in Albuquerque.

My mom was proud of us. She'd watch us play with tears of joy, but the last thing she wanted was for her sons to be musicians. She gave my dad a hard time, telling him that we needed to go to school, but he couldn't see paying musicians when he had two sons. He'd say, "We need the money. We've got bills to pay, groceries to buy." Money was important, but passion was important too. My mom says, "Music was in his blood. It was a gift from God."

We were driven to get good, but we were rewarded. If people appreciate your talent, they'll pay for it. By the time I got into middle school, I was well-off. It wasn't that I was rich—my brother and I shared a room—but I had everything I wanted, especially new clothes and Converse sneakers. As far as we were concerned, there was no other shoe. Your only choice was a no-name brand or Converse. If you wore Converse, you were in style and hip.

Whatever I got paid, I didn't see. That was for us—the family. I didn't know about making money. I played because I had to play with my father. He wouldn't say, "Here's your paycheck, son." I had to play four or five hours. That's how it was.

"Donny always gave me his money to save. He had quite a bank account by the time that he got to be eighteen or nineteen—more than nine thousand dollars," my mom remembers. "They'd play for forty or fifty bucks a night. My husband always gave them an equal amount. Jimmy wanted to spend his money. He had a girlfriend. Donny wanted to see how much he could build up."

My dad was always one step ahead. He taught my brother and me that when you play a show, people were paying to see you play. He'd work the room before he even got on stage. He'd walk around, shaking people's hands, and telling them, "Thank you for coming to see us." That made people comfortable. I do that today. It's good karma. It shows humility.

Our shows opened with a polka. It would always be instrumental. Then, after another instrumental polka, my dad would sing a song. I remember one—"Adelita." It's been around since the Mexican Revolution. It's about someone leaving Adelita to go to war. He wants to marry her before he goes off to fight.

My dad featured me in the middle of the set. I was so small that, when he announced me, people would move up to the stage to watch me sing. They'd clap and throw coins at my feet. I'd get another bag of chips and more beef jerky.

We played a variety of music. That's where I get my versatility. My dad would say, "There are young folk here. They want to hear 'La Bamba,' 'Wooly Bully,' 'Blueberry Hill,' an Elvis Presley tune, and 'The Twist.'" That was our rock & roll repertoire. We'd rock out and people would dance what my dad called "the jitterbug."

I remember another dance, the Paul Jones, that people requested at senior citizen centers. Men formed a circle on the outside, women a circle on the inside. Somebody had a whistle. When they blew it, the band played a polka. Women held hands and walked to the right while men held hands and walked in the opposite direction. When the whistle blew again, everyone grabbed a partner and danced. Anyone left without a partner sat down. They kept doing it until it wound down to only a few men and women.

My dad was a big Bob Wills & the Texas Playboys fan, so we played "San Antonio Rose." We both loved Hank Williams, so we did "Your Cheatin' Heart." I started getting into Hank Williams Jr. in high school. I listened to "real" country musicians—George Jones, Johnny Cash, Willie Nelson, Merle Haggard, and Waylon Jennings. When keyboards came into country music, it didn't appeal as much to me. What happened to the beauty of two-step country?

I couldn't wait until the band took a break. My dad would give me a dollar and I'd make my way to the bar. I'd buy potato chips and a piece of beef jerky for half a dollar. The bartender would give me a Roy Rogers for a quarter. My uncle used to be a bartender. He'd make me Shirley Temples, but I wanted a Roy Rogers now. A Shirley Temple is a Sprite with a cherry. A Roy Rogers is a Coke with a cherry. I'd sit at the edge of the bar, sipping my drink, while my dad talked to people or took a cigarette break outside. I'd use the quarter I had left to play pinball until hearing my dad on the microphone, calling me to get back onstage.

Late nights were the norm. I was just a kid, but we often played until two or three in the morning—way past my bedtime. I'd sit on an amp with my head down, fighting sleep, but I'd keep the beat. My dad would give me a look, people would be dancing, but I didn't care; I was tired. My dad would give my arm a little pinch. "Okay, I'm wide awake. Let's go." I'd last another fifteen or twenty minutes.

When it was nearing the time for people to have their last glass of beer, my dad would say, "We've got work tomorrow," and play popular songs. People would stick around and dance.

I'd be so tired by the time the band finished that I'd go to the van, sometimes, and turn the heater on and fall asleep. It's always cold in New Mexico. My dad, brother, and uncle would pack up the PA system. The next thing I'd know would be my mom trying to wake me. I didn't want to get up. I wanted to sleep. My mom remembers, "I had a hard time getting Donnie to go to school. Jimmy could handle the lack of sleep, but Donnie was younger. During breaks, he'd put his head down, cross his arms on a table, and fall asleep. Then it would be time to get back on stage and play some more."

Even when we were home, there would almost always be a jam going on. After dinner, my dad or my brother would pick up an accordion and say, "Grab your bajo sexto." We played polkas and sang songs while we ate dessert.

On Sundays, my aunts and uncles would come over. Jimmy and I would still be sleeping—totally conked out. My dad would wake us. "C'mon, I want you to play a song." Dad was a military man. When he said, "Get up," he'd only tell you once. If he told us a second time, we'd get pinched or slapped. I played with tears in my eyes sometimes, trying to sing while sucking up the tears, but I took a real liking to music, especially the sound of the accordion with the bajo sexto cranking behind it.

TWO

FLACO

Jimmy and I listened to other conjunto musicians—Tony De la Rosa, Narciso Martínez, Valerio Longoria—but they didn't have very wide repertoires. Flaco Jiménez did. He could play a tune like Esteban Jordan's "Squeeze Box Man," which reminded me of Little Richard's "Lucille," and really jam it out on the accordion. He was so cool. As my brother Jimmy says, "Flaco's the king. His style, his beat, and his heart."

Born Leonardo Jiménez on March 11, 1939, Flaco has had an illustrious career: six Grammy Awards and a Grammy Lifetime Achievement Award. He received a National Heritage Fellowship from the National Endowment for the Arts in 2012, the highest honor bestowed on an artist. He's been inducted into the *Austin City Limits* Hall of Fame, the Conjunto Music Hall of Fame, the Tejano Roots Hall of Fame, the National Hispanic Hall of Fame, and the Grammy Hall of Fame. Flaco played on Dwight Yoakam and Buck Owens' chart-topping Hot Country single "The Streets of Bakersfield" in 1988 and the Mavericks' "All I Ever Do Is Bring Me Down" in 1995. He recorded with Peter Rowan, Ry Cooder, Bob Dylan, the Rolling Stones, Doug Sahm, the Texas Tornados, Los Super Seven, and me. His album *Partners* (1992) featured guest appearances by Dwight Yoakam, Stephen Stills, Linda Ronstadt, Los Lobos, and Emmylou Harris. Flaco claims, "I've done so many sessions, I can't remember all of them. I did a record with Hank Thompson and Bekka Bramlett ['I Picked a San Antonio Rose'] in 1997, but I don't remember doing it. I listened to it and, sure enough, there's my accordion. I didn't meet them in person, but I overdubbed my accordion."

Spontaneity is at the heart of Flaco's playing. "I never plan what I do," he reports. "Sometimes I'll do a really nice lick and the recording people will want me to do it again for safety reasons. I can't do it again, not even close. I don't phrase the same licks the same way. I just respond to the song. Automatically, it comes to my mind what fits. If you feel the song, you know what to do."

He continues, "When I recorded 'The Streets of Bakersfield,' Pete Anderson was the producer. Before we recorded, he told me, 'Play your ass off.' Okay. They let the tape run. I started playing my ass off, but I misunderstood and he stopped me. I was killing the song. I was doing so many flashy things, they didn't fit. Pete said, 'A little more laid back.' Okay, now I knew what I was going to do."

Flaco represents the third generation of accordion players in his family. His grandfather, Patricio Jiménez, who died before Flaco was born, frequented German dances in New Braunfels, Texas, and was inspired to take up the accordion. "My dad used to tell me stories about my grandfather," Flaco says. "He started playing German polkas on a one-row accordion and jumped to a two-row Hohner. My dad learned polkas from my grandfather."

The first conjunto accordionist in San Antonio to record, Flaco's father, Don Santiago "Tiago" Jiménez Sr. (1913–1984), developed the Tex-Mex duet singing style with his disciple Fred Zimmerle. His debut single, "Dices Pescao" backed with "Dispensa el Arrempujón," was released by Decca in 1936. He went on to write many classic tunes. Los Lobos covered "Ay Te Dejo en San Antonio." It was heard in the film *Revenge* in 2017. The Texas Tornados performed it on *Austin City Limits*. Flaco's brother, Santiago Jiménez Jr., recorded it on his own and with Los Cenzontles. Los Texmaniacs redid it for the album *Texas Towns & Tex-Mex Sounds*. Documentary filmmaker Les Blank featured the senior Jiménez and his sons in his 1976 cinematic study of borderland music, *Chulas Fronteras*. Flaco also appeared in Blank's *Del Mero Corazón* (1979).

Don Santiago Jiménez Sr. recorded for Chris Strachwitz's Arhoolie Records in 1979, accompanied by Flaco on bajo sexto and Juan Viesca on standup bass. In 2001, Arhoolie combined contemporary tracks with tunes recorded in 1937 and released them on CD as *First and Last Recordings*. Santiago Jr. made his career an homage to his father. Inducted into the Tejano Music Awards Hall of Fame in 1993, he received an NEA National

Flaco Jiménez and
Max Baca, 1975

Heritage Fellowship in 2012. The Texas Conjunto Music Hall of Fame inducted him a year later.

Flaco began tinkling with his father's accordion when he was six or seven. He explains, "I'm self-taught. By observing my father's playing, I picked up the instrument. He didn't know I was playing. He had a day job with a cement company on the north side of San Antonio. We were a poor family, living in the barrio. We had a wood stove. My father got exceptionally low income, but he worked day and night and played music on the weekends. When he went to work, I picked up the accordion. He didn't know about it."

One day, Flaco's father got off from work early. In Flaco's words, "When he approached where we lived, he heard somebody playing his accordion, but he didn't have a clue who it was. When he opened the door, he kept it semi-closed. I didn't see him. He was hiding, listening to what I was playing. It was a surprise to him, but I played every polka he knew. By watching him, I had learned to play. He opened the door fully and caught me off guard. I didn't have a chance to set the accordion down. He wasn't a bad father—he never spanked us—but we respected him. I set the accordion to the side. There were tears all over my father's face. He embraced me. It was real satisfaction and pride. He said, 'Mijo, you can use my accordion whenever you want.' I said, 'Thank you,' and started playing and playing and playing. He was proud."

Flaco also learned chords from the guitar player in his father's group. He recalls, "I wasn't too interested in the guitar, but I heard records by Narciso Martínez and other accordionists who used a bajo sexto player and I learned to play it. I didn't master it, but I learned enough to record with my father."

Jiménez Sr. was the original Flaco, which translates as "Skinny." "When he started recording," Flaco explains, "he used the name 'El Flaco.' In 1948, he changed his band's name to Santiago Jiménez y Sus Valedores. At the time, I was just Leonardo Jiménez. I had a local band and my dad said, 'Why don't you start recording under my nickname?'"

Flaco's father persuaded Hymie Wolf, owner of the independent San Antonio-based Rio Records, to record his son's band, Los Caminantes. Flaco recalls, "My first recording as Flaco Jiménez was in 1956. I was a sideman in Los Caminantes with Henry Zimmerle (bajo sexto), Roberto Cadena (vocals), Roger Herrera (drums), and Mike Garza (bass)." A year later, Flaco formed his own group: "We played in San Antonio and Corpus Christi. It wasn't long tours. I didn't have to travel too far."

Drafted in 1952, Flaco served two years with the United States Army during the Korean crisis, then picked up his musical career where he left off. For the remainder of the 1950s and early '60s, he recorded for independent labels, including José Morante's Norteño and Sombrero Records. After recording engineer Salomé Gutiérrez and his wife opened the Del Bravo Record Shop in San Antonio in 1966, he recorded for their D.L.B. Records. He'd go to the studio, roll the tape and, in a couple of hours, record fifteen or twenty songs in the traditional conjunto style. Sometimes, there wouldn't be drums, just bajo sexto and accordion. "It was just rancheras, waltzes, and polkas, not much singing," Flaco remembers.

Later, the accordionist took a more modern approach with Joey López's Joey Records and its sublabel Dina Records. He had a big hit in 1983 with "El Pantalon Blue Jean," a comic polka that his dad had written, singing in Spanish about girls getting on a bus wearing blue jeans, going to the movies where everyone's wearing blue jeans, and finally going to a wedding where even the priest is wearing blue jeans. I was sixteen when it came out. Not long afterward, Switzerland-based Sonet Records packaged it with other tunes Flaco had recorded for Joey Records and released *Doug Sahm & Augie Meyers Present Flaco Jiménez y Su Conjunto: Tex-Mex Breakdown*.

"I thought that it was always just going to be a local thing," Flaco told the *Los Angeles Times*. "I'd only hear my dad and other groups in San Antonio or even here just in the barrio. I think that audience started changing when I began to 'bilingual' a lot of stuff and started playing rock 'n' roll and with a little country to it. Then the reaction of the people, not just the Chicanos but the Anglos, was stronger."[1]

He continued, "Instead of someone just saying, 'Oh, there goes another Tex-Mex accordion player, it has gained more respect because of the exposure it has gotten. This type of music and this instrument for years was just classified as a party joke. An accordion? Now it's a different story. Everyone wants an accordion. It took somebody to introduce it, and I'm lucky it was me who got to say, 'Listen to this blend with the Stones or Dwight Yoakam.' People say, 'I didn't know.' Well, now you know."[2]

I first heard Flaco when I was seven. My brother Jimmy says, "My dad was watching news on TV, so I went into our bedroom and put on the TV there. I flipped channels until I came to PBS. *Austin City Limits* was on. I heard the accordion. Flaco and his band were playing their asses off—on national TV! I got excited. I ran into my dad's room. He was watching the news, but I changed the channel—'Hey man, what are you doing?'—but my mom and dad loved it." My mother adds, "I called my mom and told her to put the TV on: there's a really good accordionist playing. I told her the channel. We heard the announcer say that it was Flaco Jiménez, but that was the end of that. We didn't know where he was from."

Three weeks passed. Then, my mom remembers, my grandmother went with a friend to Amarillo. "On their way back, they listened to a Tejano music program on the radio. The DJ announced that Flaco would be in Lubbock, Texas, about five hours away, the following weekend. She got home and called my husband. He got on the phone and called the hall where Flaco was playing, El Fronterizo. Sure enough. We packed up the kids on Friday and took off for Lubbock."

("I didn't understand why," says Jimmy. "I figured we could see Flaco on TV. What did I know?")

The converted auction hall—"an old barn," says my mom—had wooden walls, a tin roof, and sawdust on the floor. Its capacity was a thousand people. In the back, where the dressing room was, there were stables for the horses they were auctioning. "There was a barnyard with cows," Jimmy recalls. Flaco sounded great. He played "Viva Seguín," one of his father's polkas. I was familiar with it. I heard Flaco's accordion, but I also heard Jesse Ponce's bajo sexto cranking and rolling. They were playing such happy melodies I was attracted right away.

Once a month, Flaco played at El Fronterizo for three nights—Friday, Saturday, and Sunday—and every night would be sold out. The auction hall would be completely packed. My mom had a little cassette tape recorder. She'd put it on the table and record the show—every time. She gave the tapes to me as a gift. You can hear people talking, shuffling as they dance, but you can also hear the music and how amazing it was. Those tapes are priceless.

Flaco Jiménez and Max Baca, Mission of San Jose, San Antonio

We went to see Flaco again a few months later, and he became friends with my father. He took a liking to my brother and me. We were his biggest fans. We used to stand by the stage and watch him play. He invited Jimmy and me to come on the stage to play a song.

"I didn't know how they played," Flaco recalls. "Max's dad said, 'Give these kids a break,' so I took a chance."

When we got onstage, Jimmy took out his accordion. I took out my twelve-string guitar. I didn't have a bajo sexto yet. I was so nervous. I didn't know what to do. I had stage fright. My brother asked me, "Are you ready?" and I said, "No, I can't do this." I didn't understand what was going on; it was so weird.

People rushed to the stage. I had never experienced anything like that before. I had been playing with my father, but never to a crowd that big.

My dad was my security blanket. He used eye contact, or nodded his head, to let me know what to do. Without him, I stood there unable to move and shaking. When he saw what I was going through, he walked onto the stage and stood next to me. From there, I was okay. Jimmy and I played and sang. People clapped and started throwing quarters and dollar bills at our feet. It was overwhelming.

"I was surprised by those kids' playing," Flaco remembers. "Right away, I could see that Max was going to do something with the bajo sexto. The bajo sexto was bigger than Max, but he had the power. We became good friends."

Whenever Flaco came to Albuquerque, he'd stay with us—that's how close we became. He says today, "I was like one of the family. There was true friendship among us. I slept in Max and Jimmy's room. I consider Max a son."

My mom and dad took us to Lubbock every time Flaco played. We had to call the owner to make sure we could get tickets. During the summer, the place didn't have air conditioning. It was so hot. Flaco and his conjunto would be onstage sweating, but their music would be so beautiful. Flaco's playing was even more of a reason to fall in love with the music. Jimmy and I were like kids in a candy store.

Flaco took my brother and me under his wing. Jimmy says, "He told us we had to get tight. There was a lot of competition for gigs. He told us to practice, practice, practice. You've got to play the accordion until your ears hurt from the noise, over and over, and your fingers hurt like a basketball player's. You've got muscles in your fingers and your hands. They've got to be strong. Your mind has to be pumping."

The first time that I saw Flaco, Jesse Ponce was playing bajo sexto. Then there was Hugo González. Finally, Óscar Téllez (1946–2002) arrived. He did all kinds of wild licks. He'd be playing with discipline and then, all of a sudden, explode with all these amazing licks. They'd come at just the right time. Everybody would turn their head and go, "Wow!" That's when I decided to be a bajo sexto player.

"Óscar Téllez became his idol," says Lorenzo Martínez. Max "took lessons from him and learned his technique. He took it to a different level." Josh Baca adds, "My uncle tries to emulate Óscar Téllez, and he does a good job, but coming from a different era, he also learned rock and blues."

When I was twelve, Flaco called me and told me to bring my bajo sexto to his show. I had just gotten the 1972 Martin Macias that my father bought me. In the late 1800s, in the Mexican state of Michoacán, a luthier started making double guitars and taught his technique to an emigrant from Spain, Martin Macias. Experimenting with thicker strings, Macias made his first bajo sexto in 1925. He wound up migrating to San Antonio in the 1940s. Today, people seek out his original bajo sextos. They have a Spanish design with rope woven around the pickguards. The bridges look Spanish; they came from Spain. That was Macias' trademark. He wanted people to know where the instrument came from. It took him a year to make each bajo sexto; they were handcrafted. His factory is still making them. It's run by Macias' grandson, George. He's making me one. I have one from his father, the full-bodied model I play.

In 1979, Flaco toured with Peter Rowan ("a really mellow guy"). Peter explains: "I was spending a lot of time in Texas, as well as playing bluegrass with fiddler Tex Logan. We had a band, the Green Grass Gringos. He was from Texas, but he was living in New Jersey. My spiritual, creative center was the Southwest. I wrote 'Land of the Navajo' in the late '60s and recorded it with Jerry Garcia, David Grisman, and Vassar Clements in [the group] Old & In the Way. When I started writing songs like 'The Free Mexican Airforce,' David Grisman said, 'There's a guy who's been playing with Ry Cooder named Flaco Jiménez.' David's very offhand, but he's actually brilliant. He said, 'You should record with this guy.' So I went to Texas, hooked up with Flaco, and recorded for [the independent label] Flying Fish. I was so tired of major labels."

I met Peter in Pojoaque, New Mexico, between Santa Fe and Los Alamos. "It's an Indian pueblo," says Peter. "There was a feed store that they turned into a dance hall called the Line Camp. We played there a lot, every three or four months. It was exciting from the point of view of the hippie fanbase, but it was lacking in the sense of the Hispanic fanbase. Flaco didn't want to try material he didn't know, but we did several tunes of his. I featured him a lot. We did 'Ojos Verdes' (Green Eyes) and 'Ojos Españoles' (Spanish Eyes). Occasionally we did the Greek tune 'Never on Sunday,' because Flaco and I met on a Sunday."

Peter recalls the night Flaco brought me to the gig. "He was the same as he is now: the same jubilant spirit." When I got to the club, I walked into the dressing room. Flaco said, "Okay, let's play." Peter looked at me and said, "Hello young man, what's your name?" "I'm Max." "What've you got there?" "It's a bajo sexto."

"He was very upfront," Peter remembers. "I asked him if he played much and he said, 'I'm playing tonight.'"

I got on stage, wearing my Flaco t-shirt, and played a few songs. Peter Rowan's band backed us up. It's wonderful to think that so many years later, Peter and I are onstage again with Los Texmaniacs and the Free Mexican Airforce.

When we met, I had no idea who he was. I was more concerned with Flaco Jiménez; that's who I had come to see. Peter had grown up in Wayland, Massachusetts, about forty-five minutes west of Boston. "I was born the Fourth of July 1941," he says. "I may not be a conduit, but at the least, I'm a sensitive antenna for American culture. I play music and move fluidly through musical cultures. If I were really serious about Tex-Mex music, I'd have to know how to play solo, by myself, Spanish songs and sing in Spanish, and play huapangos and cumbias. I'm in the position of riding on the great waves that those guys create. They love me riding the waves and I'm so grateful for it."

An early rock & roll fan, Peter played Buddy Holly, Chuck Berry, and Elvis Presley tunes in a high school band, the Cupids. Mentored by bluegrass mandolinist/high tenor vocalist Joe Val, guitarist Jim Rooney, and banjo player Bill Keith, he haunted a Boston bluegrass club, the Hillbilly Lounge, and became one of the first northerners to play with Bill Monroe & the Bluegrass Boys (1964–1967). "It was acoustic, yet hard-driving," he told the magazine *Bluegrass Unlimited* in 1997, "with the great ballads, the old story songs, love songs, and strictly straight-ahead blues."[3]

Despite having the blessing of the Father of Bluegrass, Peter temporarily left hill-country music, joining Grisman in a Boston-based psychedelic rock band called Earth Opera. But bluegrass' hold was too strong for him to stray for long. In 1969, he teamed with Richard Greene in the band Seatrain; four years later, he and the Los Angeles–born fiddler formed a bluegrass supergroup, Muleskinner, with Grisman, Bill Keith, and Clarence White (The Kentucky Colonels, The Byrds). Following White's tragic death in July 1973, he helped to form Old & In the Way.

Peter has been incredibly prolific. His twenty-seven albums (as of 2020) include solo recordings and appearances with Peter Rowan's Bluegrass Band, Peter Rowan's Big Twang Theory, Peter Rowan's Twang 'n' Groove, Peter Rowan & Crucial Reggae, the Free Mexican Airforce, Druhá Tráva, the Nashville Bluegrass Band, Steve Earle, Don Edwards, Tony Rice, Jerry Douglas, and

Max Baca and Flaco Jiménez

Danny Thompson. He joined his brothers Chris and Loren for a trio album, *Tree on a Hill*, in 1994. He explains, "I'm devoted to the creative aspects that I find in myself. I have what feels like a gift to enjoy a variety of things. I love the formalities of the music—the details of rhythms—but people interpret them in different ways. It's always great to meet somebody who knows the real essence. Flaco and I recorded 'Break My Heart Again' with a wonderful bajo sexto player from San Antonio, Jesse Ponce. I found out from Max that Jesse was also a solo singer and accordion player. He was a presence. I had a sense of bolero from pop music and rock & roll. It came into mainstream music as Latin rhythms from Cuba."

Peter's bands had mandolin, guitar, and bass players. Sometimes he'd have a drummer. Flaco was on the accordion. "We toured mostly in England in the 1980s," says Peter, "until I moved to Nashville and the whole thing with Mark O'Connor and Jerry Douglas began to be fluent in terms of reaching the growing bluegrass audience. I was always able to do solo gigs in the Northeast, but England had culture vultures. They had all-White bands with sophisticated, middle-class kids reproducing music from Africa. The English have a great sense of humor. They call things like that a 'one-off.' The musicians know they're not going to make their life's career out of it, but, in their college years, they're having fun. It's a funny culture that way, but they love authenticity. When real bands show up, they pack the halls. They did that for me and Flaco and the Free Mexican Airforce."

Because he had built an earlier following in England as a solo folk artist, shows were billed under Peter's name, but the emphasis was on Flaco and the band. Peter remarks, "To British critics, I looked like one of those culture vultures. 'Why's this bluegrass guy playing Tex-Mex music?' I was criticized by one reporter and got a nasty comment from someone else. Our tour manager explained it to me. He said, 'Peter, you just don't have the "Spic" appeal.' I thought that was the worst thing I ever heard anybody say."

"The English are very race conscious," he continues. "They conquered the world as White people. Their conquerees were Brown. They looked at Flaco as though he were representative of this Mexican migration to the United States. They wanted to make him into a cultural hero defining the empire, a rebel against the White establishment, but Flaco said, 'I'm not that guy. I'm Tejano. My granddad was German. He married my grandmother in the United States. They didn't migrate.' The whole idea of origins and authenticity is a huge cultural burden. It's still showing up in this racist stuff we're going through with White supremacy and border walls. Flaco said, 'I play music.' It was a meeting of European music and Indigenous rhythms and Latino culture, which, of course, was influenced by Spain. Flaco's not playing the card that he's more authentic than you. They were rough on me as a Caucasian. Ry Cooder did it very carefully and pulled it off, but it was not something easily sustainable."

Peter returned to his bluegrass roots, but "dipping into Tex-Mex music wasn't a lark or a pastime. It wasn't a gimmick. It was because Flaco and I met, played music, and fell in love. We were spiritual consorts. Flaco was never anything other than totally into it. Any touring aggregate begins to feel its own weight. As Flaco took over the European market, I was glad for him. Once he conquered England, he went to Holland and Spain. With the Texas Tornados, he toured and toured."

Flaco may have slowed down a bit, but he's still creating great music. Playing with him is a true joy.

THREE

CRECIENDO
(Growing)

I was a hipster, a Mexican hippie. I listened to German polkas, Norteño music, and Tex-Mex music, but my friends listened to rock & roll and I had to be hip. I became a fan of Stevie Ray Vaughn, Carlos Santana, Eric Clapton, and B. B. King. You could tell when they were playing, pinpoint it as soon as you heard it. They created their own style, never imitating anybody.

Creedence Clearwater Revival was my all-time favorite rock & roll band. I dug the groove they had; they laid it down every tune. I love the beat of a solid groove. They were simple songs; I could understand John Fogerty's lyrics. The Beatles were happening, of course, but I wasn't too much of a Beatles fan. I liked "I Want to Hold Your Hand," but I was more intrigued by their voices than their groove. They didn't appeal to me the way that Creedence did. Creedence was a powerhouse. They had "Proud Mary," "Lodi," and songs like that . . . "Midnight Special" and "Bad Moon Rising."

I've dreamed of being on stage with Eric Clapton, playing right beside him, switching off on solos, riffs, and licks. Maybe someday it'll come true. I can imagine it. That would be the ultimate. I've gotten to play with Ry Cooder, Carlos Santana, and Jerry Douglas. I've shared stages with Delbert McClinton and Bill Kirchen. He's one my favorite guitarists. I had him sign my bajo sexto.

I met Taj Mahal when I was with the Texas Tornados, but we didn't talk until we were backstage at the Rhythm & Roots Festival in 2018. He asked about Óscar Téllez and I told him how he had been my idol. "Óscar was a magician," he said, "and an amazing bajo sexto player. You're close to him." That was a real compliment. He asked if he could check out my bajo sexto, so I handed it to him. He asked if it was a Macias. He figured out some chords and played.

Flaco and I played with the great blues guitarist B. B. King at the Palomino Club in North Hollywood, California, in the early 1990s. The Texas Tornados were playing a show with him and Los Lobos. Flaco and I were jamming backstage, warming up, when B. B. King walked into the dressing room and went, "Wow, that was great. Do you want to play a song with us?" Flaco said, "Sure, what key?" When we finished our set, B. B. King was getting ready to play. He invited us again to come up. We jammed on a blues tune. I got to take a solo. It was an honor.

Pedal steel guitarist Robert Randolph is a monster. He can rock out with anyone. I've always admired his music. We got to play together at Los Lobos' Lobo Fest at the Greek Theater in Los Angeles. They invited him, along with Josh and me. We got on stage and each of us did a solo—David Hidalgo and Cesar Rosas of Los Lobos, Josh on accordion, and me. Robert Randolph was in the forefront. It was so great.

Saxophonist/flute player Tony Campisi was one of my favorite jazz musicians. I used to see him on Mondays at a jam session he ran. Anyone could play. I used to go to a jazz club in Austin, the Elephant Room, and watch him play. It was hardcore jazz.

The only time I saw my mom and dad dance was when my brother and I played at fiestas or special occasions like family gatherings, but my mom loved to dance.

She and my dad spoke Spanish. My dad would say, "Learn to speak Spanish and be proud of your culture." I tried speaking Spanish as much as I could, but it wasn't until I was in my teens that I really started speaking it. As a kid, I didn't understand it. You didn't want to speak Spanish at school. People made fun of you—"You're Mexican!" I wanted to be cool and blend in with everyone.

There were Native American populations inhabiting what is now New Mexico before the influx of Europeans. Texas, New Mexico, Arizona, and California were part of Mexico. The same people were running around the same land. After their arrival in the late fifteenth century, Europeans bred with the Natives—Spaniards, British, Germans, and others. My grandmother had Spanish and Native blood. That's why she had a light complexion and blue eyes like me.

Once the border was put up, it changed everything. Suddenly, you were Mexican because you were south of the border and American Indian because

left to right Flaco Jiménez, Max Baca,
David Jiménez, and Óscar Téllez

you were on the northern side. But the border is nothing but a river—the Rio Grande. On both sides, it's the same folks: Apaches, Cheyenne, Sioux, and so on. The military tried to segregate the Native Indians so they could claim the land.

Except for a few instances, I didn't experience prejudice growing up, but about twenty years ago, I was playing with the band and we went to a restaurant. It was packed, but we were the only Mexicans there. It was a Sunday; I'll never forget it. The hostess asked us, "How many?" and we told her, "Six." She told us to wait a few minutes. We were waiting, waiting, and waiting. There were plenty of empty tables. We kept asking about them, but she kept telling us they weren't open. Finally, after the place cleared out, she sat us down. I started thinking something wasn't right.

When we were kids, we'd get into a fight and, right away, be called a "spic" or "white trash." I'd hear about the Ku Klux Klan, or see riots on TV, and wonder, "Why are we doing this? We're all the same." It was just the way it was back then. Freddy Fender told me that when he was a kid, he couldn't sit in the front of a bus. Blacks and Mexicans had to sit in the back. There were restaurants that wouldn't serve them. "Whenever I run into prejudice," Freddy told the *Washington Post* in 1977, "I smile and feel sorry for them, and I say to myself, 'There's one more argument for birth control.'"[1]

I went to Saint Therese Catholic School from the first grade through the eighth. It was difficult. Other students would see me playing Spanish music, conjunto music, or Tex-Mex music, or just playing the bajo sexto, and laugh. "What's that pregnant guitar?" They'd tell me to play Ozzy Osbourne and Grand Funk Railroad. I loved that music, but how do you tell someone that this was part of my culture? They didn't get it and they made fun. It was hard to get accepted until the *Albuquerque Journal* ran a headline, "Duke Home City Boy Makes It to the Rolling Stones," on its front page. That was awesome. I started getting phone calls from friends at school. They were just blown away. They couldn't believe it. All those years of playing my "pregnant guitar" paid off.

My dad voted Republican. When Pietro Domenici, who'd serve as United States Senator from 1973 to 2009, ran for governor in 1970 against ex–New Mexico Speaker of the House Bruce King, my dad was his campaign manager. He had experienced so much racism that he thought that, if he got into politics, it might make life easier for him.

I try to get along with everyone, give everything a chance. Everyone has a right to believe what they choose to believe, whether it's religion, music, or opinions. There's beauty in every person. I seek the positive in whatever I do. We're all the same—the same heart, the same legs, the same creator. A person might have a dark complexion, or slanty eyes, but I've learned to appreciate people and different cultures. That's been my education: hands-on training, the experience that no one could teach you. It took years, but I learned.

I went to a show in Argentina. There was an accordion player playing tangos with his son. They sounded so beautiful. Dancers came onstage and danced to their music. Trays of food were brought to everyone's table. Music, dancing, and food—every culture has that.

I remember being chased around the school by one of the nuns. I was in the second grade. We were at recess when I took a leak behind a tree. I had seen my dad do it when we were hunting at our ranch in Truth or Consequences, New Mexico. One of the girls in my class saw me and told a nun. She got her paddle out and chased me around the school three times. Finally, the bell rang. The nun was still chasing me. She couldn't catch me. I was too fast for her, but I started thinking, "What am I going to do now? I'm supposed to be in class."

I had to give up. I got hauled to the office. They paddled me three times and called my mom. She and my dad laughed about it, but to the nun, it was a serious offense. By the time my mom got to the school, I was in tears and my butt was sore.

The nun came from southern Mexico. She taught Spanish, but she loved music. When I was in the third grade, she saw me playing with my dad. The school hired him to play at a fiesta. The next day, she announced, "We have a musician in the class. I didn't know we had such a talented student." She made me get up and go to the front of the room. The class clapped for me. Then she made me sing a song. I didn't want to do it. I was put on the spot and felt embarrassed, but she pulled out some maracas from a drawer of her desk and started playing. It made me comfortable and I sang. I got an "A" for that class. That sister was cool.

There was a talent show and she told me to sign up. I got some friends who went to school with me and put a band together. We'd get together at my house after school and play. My dad had a room where his band rehearsed. There was a drum set, amplifiers, and microphones. I played guitar. Eric got on the bass, Steven got on the drums, and we started playing. I told Steven, "Play this beat." I showed him how to hold the sticks. I told him, whatever you do, don't stop until I tell you to stop. I told Eric what to play on the bass. Then I got on the guitar and started playing [the melody of "La Bamba"]. We practiced until it was time for the talent show. We ended up taking second place. They gave us an award. When I graduated from the eighth grade, they roasted us. They said, "Good luck in high school, Max Baca. We predict that you're going to be the leader of a big brass band."

When I was in the sixth grade, my dad put music to the side and focused on supporting his family with a "real job." He invested wisely and had rental income and money from selling the bar. He saw that Jimmy and I had music inside of us and became our manager.

My brother and I had always played together but it was our band now. We got a bass player and a drummer. Sometimes we couldn't get a drummer, so I played drums. Other times, I played bass.

My dad helped us raise the money for our first album, *Mi Primer Amor* (My First Love), in 1980. We recorded it on cassette at Altavista Studio. Jimmy was eighteen. He remembers, "We did a cumbia, a ranchera, and a couple of polkas. I didn't know about a lot. I was a young guy with daddy taking care of the bill. I just went to play the accordion and screw around with women. I played my ass off and whored around. I didn't have to worry; my dad had it covered."

My middle school years were the most important in my growing up; I learned so much. When I got into high school, it was a whole other world. I heard students cursing and saw them smoking and making out in the locker room.

In Catholic school, I had been taught manners and discipline. I knew not to talk when elders were speaking, but I got into my share of trouble. My eighth-grade teacher made me stay after class one day and write the word "responsibility" a thousand times. She thought it'd get through to me, but I just wanted to go home to practice. I enjoyed music, English, and art classes—loved drawing, painting, and doing pottery—but I hated P. E. and math and couldn't wait to get out of school.

We recorded Augie Meyers' "Hey Baby (Qué Pasó?)" on our second album in 1985. He had done it on his 1971 album *The Western Head Music Co.* Our record reached number one in New Mexico. We sold over ten thousand copies and got a lot of airplay. Augie says, "When I found out that they recorded my song, I called their dad and said, 'Y'all recorded my song and didn't give me credit.' He told me, 'We didn't know who wrote it.' 'Well, you should have looked on my record—it's there!'" My dad got in touch with the printer and had it corrected for the next pressing.

I took over our booking, trying to get better gigs. We were getting $200 a night for the whole band. We drove out of town, so we had to consider fuel and hotel rooms. We could get a room for twenty bucks, but by the time we were done paying expenses, we might have $100 to split. It was a good life, but it was tough.

FOUR

LA MÚSICA
(The Music)

When I play, every night is different. I can't repeat the same lick every time. I can't do modern commercialized stuff. I mean, I *could* do it, but I choose not to. It doesn't fit my switch. I like to play for people in the moment. I learned that way. I recorded my first album with my dad when I was twelve years old. We just went into the studio. There was no "Stop at the third verse and do this arrangement." Hell no! It was more "Let's have fun, create a positive vibe, and play beautiful music."

During Los Texmaniacs shows, I give a brief history of our music and talk about how the Europeans influenced it. The polka comes from Poland. The accordion comes from Germany, though there were accordion-like instruments in Italy, Romania, and Austria. Europeans who settled in Texas brought diatonic button accordions. It was the first time the local people had heard them; there were no accordion factories in Mexico or the United States before.

Tejano accordionists had a different feel; they weren't European. They couldn't understand what the Germans were singing, but they could understand their melodies, which were catchy. They added their own accents and spice. Everything was instrumental; there were no lyrics.

On June 11, 1930, Roberto Rodríguez became the first accordion player to record in the conjunto style. He wasn't asked to record again. The next day, OKeh Records recorded Bruno Villareal, a partially blind accordion player from La Grulla, Texas, who billed himself as "El Azote del Valle" (the Scourge of the Valley). He continued to record for the New York–based label for years.

Bajo sexto strings are brass-wound; they resonate and ring. They're bright and crispy, kind of like the strings inside a piano. The oud, from the Middle

East, also has twelve strings and a neck that's bent back, and it's tuned the same as a bajo sexto. They were probably the first guitars. They spread to Spain where the Spaniards modernized them.

I started playing bajo sexto when I was seven. I didn't have a bajo sexto yet, but I had a twelve-string guitar that I tuned like a bajo sexto. My dad bought me my first bajo sexto when I was nine. He bought it in a cantina in Juárez, Mexico, for twenty-five dollars. It was hanging behind the bar. My dad asked who owned it and the bartender said, "It's mine." "Would you sell it?" "No, it's not for sale, but give me fifty bucks." My dad offered him twenty-five. That was my first bajo sexto. It's on display in the Musical Instrument Museum in Phoenix, Arizona.

Growing up, Jimmy and I were the best of friends. We stuck together like peanut butter and jelly. He was my partner; I'll always love him. We sang together, played accordion and bajo sexto together. We dreamed of making it, of having a famous Conjunto and playing big shows. We were kids playing in nightclubs and bars. There were times when my dad couldn't make a gig, so my brother had to be my guardian. We had a notarized document acknowledging it.

Jimmy could sing; he's got a great voice. He was a better singer than me. He sang like a bird. He could carry a tune and stay on pitch. It was easy to follow him. My mom remembers, "Their voices together were great."

Jimmy's influences were Flaco and my dad, who taught him to play, but he had his own style. He learned on the accordion that my dad learned on, but then he got a two-and-a-half-row semi-chromatic Club II-b accordion. He was probably the best accordion player in the state. When people needed an accordion player, he was first call. One time, a Mexican singer who had hit songs, Juan Gabriel, was touring with a mariachi extravaganza. He had a fifteen-piece orchestra, but his accordion player couldn't make a gig. They asked for a recommendation and my brother's name came up. He got to play. He was familiar with the songs; they were so popular. We even played a few as the Baca Brothers.

At first, we had a crude sound system without monitors. We didn't mic the drums. The PA was two columns of speakers and a small four-channel mixing board. I started learning more and more about sound, going to music stores and buying this or that.

We were invited to play at fiestas. There was one about three and a half

La Música (The Music)

hours south of Albuquerque, right before you get to Truth or Consequences, the town named after the TV show. From there, you head up into the mountains. I'm talking cactuses and dirt roads, one lane, with tire marks. We were driving to the gig when we came to a small creek. It was just a trickle of flowing water. It was no problem to cross this creek; we just drove through it. We headed down this long dirt road and came to a church, Santa Rita, made of adobe. It was five or six in the evening. There were hundreds of tents. Some campers told the band to "come and eat." It was really good food.

As we started setting up our gear, we noticed that the skies were overcast. It looked like we were in for some rain, but we weren't worried about it. We were going to be playing in a big tent. They had a generator because there was no electricity. The skies kept getting darker. It started drizzling. We didn't realize it, but there was a storm coming from the north. When we started playing, it started sprinkling a little harder. It continued all evening. More and more people came into the tent. We were playing and people were dancing, kicking up dust, and having a good old time.

Back then, we'd play from six at night until three in the morning. We would play an hour, take a break, then play for another two hours. My dad would play a little with us, and then we'd take another break. By midnight, it was raining bad. We stopped playing after someone said, "There's a flash flood."

The little rio had barely been an inch of water when we went over it. Now it was gushing. It was dangerous, a roaring flood ten or fifteen feet deep. The state police were there, but nobody was going to cross the rio. There was no way. People were worried. That was the only way to get out. We were surrounded by canyons and mountains. Not even a four-wheel drive could get in or out. We were stranded.

We didn't know what to do. The band had come in our van. My dad had come in his truck with my mom, my aunts, my sister Margaret, my nephew Jacob, and my son, who was six at the time. We had no clue that this was going to happen, and we were unprepared. We packed into the only place where we could keep warm, the church. By this time, a cold front had come through. It started snowing, blizzard-y weather.

Some people had sleeping bags. Others were sleeping in the pews: they were packed. We had to find a place to lie down. We were so tired. Jimmy and a couple of the guys in the band slept in the van, with the motor running. It was bitterly cold. The storm wasn't letting up. By this time, it was three or

Los Hermanos Baca

four in the morning. We gathered by the altar, packed together like a can of sardines, and tried to sleep. Some Natives were praying.

In the morning, my dad went to look at the creek. There was no way to get out. We were stuck there for two nights. A Red Cross helicopter brought food and blankets.

My dad could be stubborn. Around noon on the second day, he got into his Chevy Silverado pickup truck with my mom, my aunts, my son, and my nephew. By now, the rio had gone down a little. Instead of ten feet, it was six feet. They were going to chance it. They started crossing the rio. They got about halfway when the truck stopped. Water got in the engine. They couldn't go anywhere. The current was strong, and the truck started to move with the water. Water was gushing against the window and started seeping into the cab. There was no way anyone could open the door, there was so much pressure. This was serious. "We almost drowned," my mom says. "Someone told my husband he could make it. They must have been joking." Carlos recalls, "We started tilting to one side. I looked at my cousin and said, 'We're going to die. This is it!'"

Thank God, there was a man on the other side of the rio with a front-end loader. He saw that my dad was in trouble. He drove that loader into the rio, stopped in the middle, and went out on the scooper with a chain. He managed to tie the chain to the bumper of my dad's truck. He was drenched but he pulled my dad to the other side. My dad's truck was history.

By now it was four or five in the afternoon. The water had gone down another couple of feet. I had to get out of there, so I said, "I'm going to take a chance and cross." I loaded the van down with our instruments. Everyone piled in and we took off down the dirt road. We made it. In another ten miles, we got to the highway.

I took guitar in seventh and eighth grade, but I couldn't understand the concept of reading music. I learned to play by listening. My ear and my heart are how I play. In high school, other musicians showed me some things. I asked them, "What's this I-IV-V?" and they explained that it was just a scale. So I started learning scales and different chords. It was another world.

If I heard something, I could play it, but it looked like chicken scratch to me. In music classes, the instructor would say, "Max, play that scale on the blackboard." Fortunately, by the time it'd get to me, everyone else in the class had played it and I had it memorized.

People were always telling me to learn to read music, that it would help my career. When I was growing up, it was always in the back of my mind. The day I moved to Austin, I was invited to participate in the recording of the soundtrack of *The Alamo* (2004), starring Dennis Quaid, Billy Bob Thornton, Jason Patric, and Emilio Echevarría. The violinist had called me and said, "Mr. Baca, we know you play the twelve-string. We'd love for you to come down to the sound studio and play." I said, "Sure" and went to Willie Nelson's studio, where they were recording. The violinist asked me about a twelve-stringed instrument that had been played in the mid-1800s. It wasn't a bajo sexto, which didn't come to Texas until the very end of the nineteenth century. He said, "It had a curved neck that bent back," and showed me a picture of a Spaniard on a horse, holding an oud. The violinist said, "Well, if it's not a bajo sexto, how about using a nylon-stringed guitar?" I agreed and grabbed a guitar. They laid all this sheet music in front of me and the director said, "Okay, Max. Here's the tempo: go ahead."

I just sat there. I couldn't read a note. I thought I had blown my big chance, but I asked if I could hear the song. "Is there anything wrong?" "I'm a little embarrassed, but I don't know how to read music." This guy comes out of the control room, grabs the sheets of manuscript paper, and says, "I'm sorry, Max. We can get anyone from the University of Austin to come and play this with sheet music. We hired you because we wanted a real human feel." I said, "If that's the case, let me hear the song."

I used a guitar from the 1800s and thought to myself how fortunate I was: Whoever said I had to read music if I wanted to get somewhere was wrong.

Music expresses feeling. How can you chart out what someone is feeling? You can't do it. You can play with a metronome, and put the right notes in the right spots, but it's not going to have a feel. It's just going to be mechanical.

FIVE

FAMILIA

(Family)

Accordions and bajo sextos are all over the place in Texas, but Los Hermanos Baca was probably the only conjunto in New Mexico. My brother booked us. We recorded seven albums together. Dad was our manager. It was a continuation of what we had been doing with our dad, but we were taking a new approach. We tried to match what was happening on the radio and keep up with the times. We played the old songs, but we added new ones too. We'd see Flaco and get inspired.

Jimmy and I played locally, but it was hard to be accepted. We were playing Tex-Mex music while other bands were playing "Mustang Sally," "Johnny B. Goode," and rock & roll. It was hard, but we stuck to our guns and started getting popular. The Baca Brothers would play a club and pack it.

Jimmy went to school all twelve years, but he's the only one in my family to graduate. He admits, "It was hard to do all that homework. All I wanted to do was play music."

In the eleventh grade, I missed a lot of school. I played so much music on the weekend that, come Monday morning and time for school, I didn't want to do it. I was just too tired. After a gig, we'd have to load the PA and drive home. By then, it'd be five or six in the morning. We were lucky to get an hour of sleep before going to school. It was tough. I promised my mother that I would get my diploma, so I took the GED test and passed. My mom was happy.

My dad had an income tax business. He did everything by hand. After he bought a computer, he couldn't figure it out. A friend had to come and program it and show him how to use it. He told me that was the future. He was on it day and night.

Ninety percent of my dad's clients were Mexican. It was easy to cross over the border and work. He wanted Jimmy and me to take the business over. We tried to do it. We took H & R Block and business classes. "He told us to keep music as a sideline," Jimmy remembers. "Otherwise, we'd starve to death. He was right. Accounting, bookkeeping, taxes—that's where the bucks are. He was well-off but he worked hard to get to a good point in life and make ends meet."

During high school, I played music on the weekends and worked at my cousin's lumberyard after school during the week. I learned so much, from types of lumber to nails, parts, and hardware. I didn't know about metric sizes or measuring tape before. It was the best education. In school, I'd sit there, trying to listen to the teacher, but it wouldn't soak into my head—math, figures, and stuff like that. I was constantly thinking about music.

I was working at the lumberyard one day when my uncle, who owned it, said, "Baca, take me to the flea market." We got in his truck and I drove him to the flea market about a half a mile down the road. It was cool; I got out of work. We were getting ready to park when he goes, "Stop right here!" There was a guy walking. His shoes were coming apart. His toes were sticking out. My uncle said, "I can't stand to see that." He was a jokester. I pulled over and he rolled down the window. "Sir, come here." The guy came over to the car. My uncle pulled out this big wad of money with a rubber band wrapped around it. He said, "Sir, let me see those shoes" and then he goes, "Here's a rubber band to hold them together." He was only kidding, of course, and he handed him a twenty-dollar bill.

My brother and I played at that flea market when we first started. My uncle's best friend from high school owned it. My uncle asked him as a favor to allow us to play. We'd play from noon until 4 p.m. on Sundays and attract people.

Los Hermanos Baca played at local cantinas, weddings and quinceañeras. We managed to record an album for a popular San Antonio label: Joey Records, the label Flaco used to record on. My dad financed the album and came with us to record. We had to go all the way to San Antonio, over seven hundred miles away, but we got a lot of radio play. Spanish stations around the country started playing our music. "Marina" was a big hit. We started getting calls to perform in California, Arizona, and Texas and appeared on syndicated Spanish-language TV shows. We were on *The Johnny Canales Show* four times. Flaco remembers, "They meshed really good. They got it from their dad, but he was more Norteño music. Donnie had the groove and knew how to use the bajo sexto the right way."

I called Juan Tejeda, a cofounder of the Conjunto Festival, in 1982. He hired bands and emceed the three nights of the festival. He's a fine accordion player and singer. His band, Conjunto Aztlan, was inducted into the Tejano Roots Hall of Fame in 2016 and the Texas Conjunto Hall of Fame a year later. They're a great band in the old-time conjunto style.

I asked what it would take to play the Conjunto Festival and he said, "I'm going to give you a chance. I'm going to book you." It was an honor . . . plus, we got paid. We drove from Albuquerque to San Antonio to play at the festival. We were nervous. We were playing conjunto music—the music we loved—and getting the chance to play it in Texas along with the pioneers we listened to. Artists on the bill were the ones we looked up to.

Eduardo Díaz, former San Antonio cultural affairs director and co-founder of the International Accordion Festival, saw us at the 1983 Conjunto Festival.

Los Hermanos Baca: Daniel Silver Jr. (guitar), Carl Lucero Jr. (drums), Jimmy Baca, Max Baca, New Mexico State Fair, 1983

He says: "I was familiar with conjunto music, but I was amazed that a band from New Mexico would be playing traditional conjunto music. They were young. They weren't Tony De la Rosa or Steve Jordan, but to Juan Tejeda's credit, he always made room for new artists or groups that weren't well known. Groups like Los Hermanos Baca played early in the day."

"Max had incredible musicianship," remembers Pat Jasper, the International Accordion Festival's artistic director for most of its thirteen-year existence (2001–2014). "He had the direct influence of important musicians who mentored him, but he was originally an outsider. That may be the key to why he saw beyond the standard frontier. Flaco did it first but Max took it to another level."

During tax season (January to April), I worked part-time for my dad, but I wanted to play music; that's all I wanted to do. I wanted to be on stage. My younger sister Maxine owns my dad's tax business now. We were close. When my brother hung out with his friends, I'd hang out with Maxine. She's called me since my dad passed in 2002 and asked for my advice. Of course, the tax business is a lot more competitive now. They used to do taxes by hand. Now, it's all electronic filing.

Jimmy was married twice. He had three kids with his first wife and two with his second, including Josh. "Before Josh was born," he says, "he would move around in his mother's belly when I played music. It must have been the vibrations. He was feeling it. When he was four, he asked me to teach him to play the accordion. I showed him scales, the way my dad taught me. He loved it. All he wanted to do was play music. When he went to kindergarten, he'd take his accordion to school. He had an ear for the music. It's his heart and soul." My mom adds, "He was in diapers and wanted to play that accordion. My husband taught him some chords."

The Thanksgiving that he was five, Josh came walking out of the kitchen playing the one-row accordion that used to belong to my grandfather. He wasn't really playing, but you could tell he had real passion for it. He loved the attention. After eating, he presented *The Josh Baca Show*. Jimmy and I looked at each other and laughed. We knew what Josh was trying to sing and play on the accordion. He knew our records and was trying to play the same licks. We knew he was going to be a musician. There was no doubt. I was living next door to my mom in one of the apartments my folks owned. Josh was always coming over, saying, "Hey, Uncle, let's jam."

Josh kept his accordion in a small ice chest. It was brilliant. One-row accordions don't come with belt straps but with thumb holes. Josh managed to get his dad's belt through the hole. He put it over his neck and through his arm. That was his strap.

I'd get my bajo sexto out; Josh would take out his accordion. I'd say, "What do you want to play?" and he'd say, "Let's play 'Marina.'" He'd tap "one, two, three" and start playing. The notes were wrong, but I could hear him trying to play the melody. He'd start singing and I'd sing with him. Then he'd say, "Let's play 'La Bamba.'" He'd be singing and trying to play the accordion—"Wooly Bully" and all these rock & roll songs, some polkas. This happened every chance Josh got. His dad, my brother, kept telling him, "Stop bothering Uncle Donny."

My mom remembers, "We'd sit in the kitchen, with Donny playing bajo sexto and Josh playing accordion. Josh would stop his uncle and say, 'You're in the wrong key.' Donny would say, 'You're right, let's do it again.' We'd laugh." "He always had the fire for music," my brother adds. "When he was a little guy, I got a webcam. I set it up and said, 'Let's do a photo shoot.' I dressed him up and he played accordion."

We brought Josh onto the stage when Jimmy and I played. He stood between us and pretended like he was playing. He was a big attraction. Jimmy says, "He got paid fifty dollars a gig. To a little boy, six or seven years old, that was a lot of money."

"Josh is amazing," says Noel Hernandez. "He can play in any key. The button accordion is a diatonic instrument, so it varies in keys. It blows my mind when I see Josh pick up an accordion with a different arrangement of notes and figure it out. He was born for that. With his energy and charisma on stage, he enlightens people. It's a great trip." Peter Rowan agrees: "Josh inherited Flaco's great lineage of musical styles, but he's also, if you don't mind me saying so, a genius of sound. As a kid, my parents would call out to me, 'That's enough, Peter.' I would be imitating all the different musical instruments that I heard—trumpet, steel guitar, accordion, ukulele, drums. I would lie in bed making those sounds. I think Josh's the same way. He's the spark of enlightenment."

"I'm so proud of my grandson," says my mom. "I told him the same thing I told my son: Do what you do and always be humble. 'I know, Grandma,' he said."

"I don't remember ever not playing the accordion," Josh says. "It was always around. Of course, as a kid, I played with toys, and threw my football outside, but I always had an accordion. My dad bought me a little one-row accordion. That was my 'box.' I wanted to be like my dad and my uncle, like my grandpa. I saw Flaco play and it blew my mind. That was it for me. I wanted to re-create the Flaco sound. I listened to all of his records."

Around that time, the movie *La Bamba* was popular. Josh loved it: "I could watch it and say every line. Lou Diamond Phillips, who played Ritchie Valens, was rocking. He was cool—a Chicano boy."

"Josh wanted to be Ritchie Valens," remembered my mom. "He'd turn up his collar and comb his hair like him."

As a Christmas present, I bought Josh a plastic electric guitar. "It was a toy," he recalls, "but it didn't matter. If I didn't have the guitar, I'd use a rake and pretend it was a guitar. Coming from a state where there was no conjunto music, nobody played accordion but my dad and grandpa. At school, my friends were listening to hip-hop, rock, and blues. My uncle and my dad would bust out Creedence Clearwater Revival tunes and conjunto songs. It was a mixture of both."

There's always a great lineup of musicians at the state fair, Expo New Mexico. The Texas Tornados headlined there in 1991. Ronnie Milsap, Ray Charles, and the Bellamy Brothers also played that year. Only two bands in the history of Tingley Coliseum, where all the big concerts are held, have ever sold out—Rick Trevino and the Texas Tornados. I mean, it was sold out to the gills—more than forty thousand people.

A few days before, Flaco called me and told me to bring my bajo sexto. Óscar Téllez hadn't made the flight. He wound up staying in Chicago for six or seven months. Nobody knew where he was. It ended up that he was staying at a bar his friend owned, playing music on the weekends and working as a bartender during the week. Flaco says of that event, "I spoke with Doug Sahm and told him we needed a bajo sexto. I said, 'Donny's the one.'" Dismissing his previous encounter with Los Hermanos Baca, Augie Meyers remembered, "Flaco brought Max in and we became good friends."

At Tingley Coliseum, the Texas Tornados—Doug, Augie, Freddy Fender, and Flaco—were driven to the stage in a convertible. People were yelling and screaming. The rest of the band followed in a pickup truck. We were driven around the arena a couple of times. People waved at us; it was so amazing.

We got on this rotating stage and started playing. I had been listening to the Texas Tornados' albums, so I knew the tunes. After the show, Flaco talked to Doug, Freddy, and Augie. "What do you think about Max finishing the tour with us? We need that bajo sexto sound." Doug said, "I don't have a problem with that."

When I got home, I told my mom and dad. My whole family was, "Oh, my God, great!" They were so happy for me. The next day, I had to fly out, so my mom took me to the store and bought me new clothes. I was going to be gone for two weeks—on tour. "We got him a Dallas Cowboys bag," says my mom, "and he took off."

I flew to San Diego; I'll never forget it. When I landed, Flaco was waiting at the baggage claim. He had a rent-a-car and drove me to the hotel. Of course, guess what hotel—La Quinta.

We played a club in San Diego, the Belly Up. Then we headed north toward Los Angeles. We stopped and played in a little town, San Juan Capistrano, at a club called the Coach House. We stayed at La Quinta.

I didn't know it, but Doug and Freddy had told the sound engineer to record the set at the Coach House. They wanted to hear my bajo sexto playing. The next day, we were supposed to leave at noon. Around 10:30, Doug, Freddy, Augie, and Flaco got together to listen to the show. They focused on how I played. Then Freddy called me to his room and said, "Don't think, just because you play the bajo sexto good, you can come and join the Texas Tornados." Then he said, "You're not even from Texas." He was putting pressure on me.

I looked at Flaco and he winked. We went into Augie's room. Doug was there. They started talking. Doug said, "We heard the show last night and think that you fit in with the band. Flaco gives you the seal of approval. That's good." Freddy looked at me and said, "Hey man, welcome to the Texas Tornados."

It was a great day, a dream come true. Here I was—a kid from New Mexico, growing up playing with my father in pueblos and bars three or four nights a week, quinceañeras, weddings, and senior-citizen centers, Jimmy and me going off on our own, playing cantinas, and, finally, me coming to San Antonio to record with my heroes.

My mom recalls, "He was so happy. They'd fly him out of here. He didn't have to go to Texas. His ticket would come in the mail or FedEx would bring it and he'd fly to wherever they were."

I started playing big venues with the Texas Tornados. During the week, we'd play in really cool clubs and theaters. On the weekends, it would be rodeos and stadiums. We played shows with the Beach Boys. We played at Bill Clinton's inaugural ball. We played country music festivals and Farm Aid with John Mellencamp, Willie Nelson, and Dolly Parton. We toured with Brooks & Dunn. We played the halftime show at an NFL football game in 1991. It was the Chicago Bears versus the Phoenix Cardinals. We played "Who Were You Thinking Of" on the fifty-yard line. It was so cool.

It was hard for me to make the decision to join the Texas Tornados and leave my brother behind. He was happy for me, but he was also sad. His musical partner was going in another direction and he felt betrayed—"there go our dreams." He continued to play locally. I'd come home and we'd talk about it. I'd say, "Brother, I'm making a move but I'm doing it for us, so someday you and I can get together. It'll get my foot in the door, but it's not going to be forever."

"I didn't blame him," Jimmy says. "I was happy that my brother could do it and make money. It's a job."

SIX

CIMA DE CARTEL
(Headlining)

When I was in high school, I liked smoking pot and getting high. One year, we played a county fair in San José. That's where I met the love of my life. The Texas Tornados were sharing the bill with Asleep at the Wheel and Willie Nelson. After the soundcheck, we went to our dressing room to get ready. We had an hour to kill before we had to get on stage. Doug Sahm asked me, "You want to groove, man?" I said, "Yeah, man." I thought he'd say, "Come to my room" and light up a joint, but he said, "Let me show you how to groove—come on."

He took me onto Willie Nelson's bus. It was the first time that I met Willie. Doug introduced us and I shook his hand. "Honor to meet you, sir." "It's my pleasure, young man."

Ray Benson (Asleep at the Wheel) was there. In a deep voice, he said, "Hi Max, how're you doing?" Doug was just talking away; he always had a good rap. He could talk and talk. Before I knew it, Willie handed me a joint. I took it. "Cool, man, yeah! I'm going to smoke with Willie Nelson." I took a good hit, almost choked to death. Then I passed it to Ray Benson. He took a hit and passed it to Doug. Then he passed it to Willie who passed it to me. Ray Benson lit another joint. The bus was full of smoke. We were laughing and talking, telling stories. All of a sudden, Doug said, "Okay Max, we've got to go." Willie shook my hand again: "Have a good show."

We got off the bus and started walking. I could see Doug's mouth moving but he was talking in slow motion. Suddenly, boom! It hit me like a ton of bricks. I was petrified, but I still had to play. They handed me my bajo sexto, and I started playing, but I had never been so stoned in my life. I was so high. I was on fire—the Stevie Ray Vaughn of the bajo sexto. Doug was high, too. He turned around and laughed. He looked at me, with his eyes bloodshot, and said, "Isn't this a groove?" "Yeah, but I don't know what key I'm playing in."

Doug Sahm could deal with record company executives. He'd see them during their lunch break and get a record deal. He knew how to talk, and he had the firepower to back it up with the musicians he chose. The Texas Tornados had a five-year deal with Warner Brothers and did three albums before I joined. I played on their final studio album, *4 Aces* (1996), and *Live from the Limo* (1999), recorded at Antone's in Austin.

Flaco's early-1980s band with Óscar Téllez, Ruben Valle (bass), and Isaac Garcia (drums) was the cream of the crop—the band that Ry Cooder used. That unit was untouchable. The first time I saw them, I made up my mind to play bajo sexto.

Laredo, Texas–born Óscar Florentino Téllez played bajo sexto on the Texas Tornados' Warner Brothers albums. He was my idol. I was impressed by his fancy licks. They were so unique and different from any other bajo sexto player's licks. His riffs were magical. They would stick out and turn heads. He played them really fast; they were so creative. Instead of the basic scale licks, Óscar did syncopated licks, right on the beat. They were so cool. He told me one time, "I'm not going to be around forever. You need to carry on the tradition of the bajo sexto and take it to the next level."

Óscar was a very disciplined musician, but he'd do a bajo sexto lick at just the right time. He'd hold off while Flaco was jamming and getting intense and then, all of a sudden, when you least expected it, he'd come up with this amazing syncopated lick. He'd play off the time, but land perfectly. He was a master. He used his mouth to imitate the sound of a trumpet and harmonized with his bajo sexto. I've never seen anyone else do that. I studied his playing—he was my idol—but he was humble, the nicest guy you could meet.

"Óscar was a Charlie Chaplin kind of guy," remembers Flaco, "really funny. He had a face like Pancho Villa, but he couldn't hurt a cat." Peter Rowan calls him "totally friendly" and says, "He was the nudge, the elbow in the ribs. You're trying to be serious on stage and he'd be right next to you, giving you a poke in the ribs, telling you, 'It's not that serious.'"

"There was nobody like Óscar," Augie Meyers recalls. "It's like Freddy

Fender. There's nobody else like him. When they were created, they broke the mold. Doug Sahm, too. Max is the same way."

"Óscar was so free with his instrument," adds Noel Hernandez. "He had all these tricks in his bag. It made me realize that people could do it with any instrument. That was the approach I wanted to take on the bass. Óscar did it so tastefully. He'd comp chords but, at the same time, sustain notes or cut them short. It created this beautiful flow so people could dance or sing along. It drove the song so well. When it came to taking solos on the bajo sexto, something that wasn't common. Óscar could do it. He'd go crazy, trilling strings and applying all kinds of other tricks. Max does that. It's really fun to back him up."

Óscar Téllez was the first bajo sexto player to tour the world, because he played with Flaco. We'd play in Spain or Holland and people would chant his name. He could look intimidating, like the Frito Bandito in a black hat, long, stringy hair and handlebar mustache, but he could play the hell out of that bajo sexto. I know bajo sexto players who have tattoos of him on their arms. That's how much he impacted them.

Óscar could be loco. He drank and did drugs. Flaco told me when they met, Óscar was going through hardship. He had split up with his wife and didn't care about life anymore. He pawned his instruments and lost his home. He lost his entire family—five sons and a daughter. It was sad.

Óscar also played with Marion, Texas–born Mingo Saldivar, "The Dancing Cowboy," but Flaco told me he was the only bajo sexto player who could cut playing with him. Óscar and Flaco were the dynamic duo. He was Flaco's right-hand man. Flaco would go looking for him and find him at a cantina drinking. Sometimes Óscar wouldn't even go home. He'd stay at the bar. He'd go in the back, lie down behind the dumpster, and fall asleep. "I found him in the dumpster," says Flaco, "but people really dug him—what he did, how he played, his features."

When we toured with Flaco, we'd be gone for three weeks or a month. We'd come home with a handful of cash. Óscar would have $10,000 or more but he didn't have a bank account. He would tip waitresses a hundred dollars. He tried to tip flight attendants, but they'd say, "We're not allowed to accept that."

One time, he was walking onto an airplane. There was a woman holding a baby in the aisle. He went up to the baby and said hello. The baby started crying. "No, no, no, don't cry!" The baby started crying more. Óscar turned to the mom, told her to "buy a present for your baby," and put a folded-up hundred-dollar bill in her hand. That's just the way he was, kind-hearted.

Óscar took a liking to me and we became good friends. He respected me as a musician. The memories that stick out came after the gigs, when we'd go back to our hotel or to a jam session.

The Texas Tornados' first album, in 1990, went double platinum. They would go into a studio, record forty or fifty songs, and Warner Brothers would pick out the best and release an album. *Zone of Our Own* came out in 1991, *Hangin' on by a Thread* a year later.

For *4 Aces*, my first album with the Texas Tornados, we recorded a whole new batch of songs. Before we recorded it, I drove with Doug and Flaco to a gig in El Paso. Freddy, Augie, and the rest of the guys flew, but Doug wanted to drive. He asked me to come and Flaco said he'd come too. Doug thought it'd be great. We could clear our minds, talk, and maybe write a song. We stopped at a roadside rest area and sat at a picnic table. Flaco drank a Miller Lite. Doug and I said, "We'll drink a beer too," so all three of us were sitting there and drinking beer. Doug said, "This is such a groove, man."

The sun was starting to go down. Doug said, "Flaco, you, Freddy, Augie, and me are like four aces." Then Flaco goes, "There's a song right there." Doug started writing. "It'll make a great video."

We never made the video, but we recorded "4 Aces." "On a midnight train to Laredo, / four aces stepped aboard / gonna find Laredo Rose, / and find out who she chose." "Laredo Rose" had been one of the hits on the first album, written by Rich Minus. The line "One had an accordion in his left, a cold beer in his right" was about Flaco. "One was a hippie completely out of sight" was Doug. "One was a border singer from San Benito they say" was Freddy, and "One had a ponytail" was Augie. "Four aces goin' nowhere, / ridin' gently towards the sun."

That was all we got before getting to El Paso and doing the show. Doug told me, "You and Flaco have to ride with me to Albuquerque." That's a three-hour drive. That's when we got the second part of the song. It ended with the four characters stepping onto this midnight train, looking for Laredo Rose, to see who she's going to choose. It turns out that she chooses Freddy, but "a bearded singer from Texas way," based on Willie Nelson, comes to kill Freddy. He wants Laredo Rose. He's going to shoot not just Freddy, but all the guys. Just as luck would have it, in enters Grateful Fred, a spoof on the Grateful Dead, and saves the day. Doug was a Deadhead, big time. He was so happy when we finished the song. It became the title track of the album.

Arlyn Studios in Austin was so huge, everybody was in a different room. Doug asked me how I liked to record my bajo sexto and I told him that I used a mic and direct box. He asked me to use an amplifier. He told me to play and said to the engineer, "I want the sound coming out of those speakers." The engineer said, "That's easy enough: we'll put a mic on it."

We were in the studio for a week, recording one or two songs a day, trying for three. We didn't start a song, put it aside, and get back to it. We finished what we started—vocals and all. If you come back to a song, you're not in the same groove as you were when you started. Doug didn't like doing that. He liked finishing a song before going on to the next one.

"4 Aces" was the first song we recorded. Doug said, "Max, I want you to do that bolero riff you do." The song starts with the bajo sexto. Augie comes in on piano, then the bass player, the drummer, and Flaco on accordion. Boom! It was magic. It's a great song.

Doug wrote "A Little Is Better than Nada," "Ta Bueno, Compadre (It's OK, Friend)," and "Clinging to You." Freddy wrote "In My Mind" and the English lyrics of Doug's "My Cruel Pain." I wrote two songs—"Mi Morenita" and "Amor de Mi Vida"—with my roommate, Louie Ortega, in San Luis Obispo. The whole time we toured with the Texas Tornados, we roomed together. We wrote a lot of songs together, but we would never finish them. I have a bunch of songs that I need to finish. Flaco helped us finish "Mi Morena." He and Freddy sang it.

Freddy sang "Amor de Mi Vida" and Doug sang a verse. We recorded Joe "King" Carrasco's "Tell Me" with Joe playing lead and rhythm guitar. He also played rhythm guitar on "A Little Is Better than Nada." Ry Cooder played slide guitar on "The Gardens" by Chris Gaffney. The roots-music magazine *No Depression* wrote that on this album, the Texas Tornados were "moving [with] casual grace and unmasked joy across the familiar Tejano territory."[1]

Doug Sahm loved California, especially northern California. That's where they grew the best weed. We'd start in San Diego and work all the way up to San Francisco, constantly on the Route 101 coastal highway up to Portland

and Seattle. From the time that I joined in 1995 until 2006, we were always on the road, selling out clubs like Slim's in San Francisco and Tipitina's in New Orleans, and traveling on our two buses.

I learned a lot by watching how Doug, Ry Cooder, and producers Don Was and Jim Dickinson recorded, just by hanging out and experiencing different recordings.

SIR DOUGLAS, AUGIE, AND FREDDY FENDER

"Doug Sahm stood out like a rock superstar," my son Carlos remembers. "He had that real cool vibe, kind of a rasp in his voice."

Born in San Antonio on November 6, 1941, Douglas Wayne Sahm was a five-year-old musical wunderkind when he debuted on a children's talent contest broadcast by radio station KMAC. He was so small that he had to stand on a chair to reach the mic. He sang "Teardrops in My Heart," written by Vaughn Horton in 1947 and recorded by the Sons of the Pioneers the same year.

Doug was soon turning heads with his triple-neck steel guitar, fiddle, guitar, and mandolin playing. His mother sent him to Bob's Music Store for guitar lessons but, within a couple of weeks, his teacher informed her that he could already play anything by ear.

After two years on the Mutual Network's *Stars Over San Antonio*, accompanied by his older brother Vic on rhythm guitar, Doug became a featured performer on the Saturday night *Louisiana Hayride*, broadcast from Shreveport's Municipal Auditorium. He got to sit in with such country artists as Hank Thompson and Webb Pierce. Offered a permanent slot on the *Grand Ole Opry*, Doug reluctantly turned it down. His mother insisted that he finish junior high school first.

Doug's father occasionally helped out at Charlie Walker's San Antonio bar, the Barn, where Hank Williams frequently performed. Doug encountered the country music legend many times. There's a great photo taken on September 17, 1952 of eleven-year-old Doug sitting on Hank's lap at the Barn. "His breath stunk of whiskey," Doug recalled, "and there wasn't nothin' left to him. He was all skinny, and his knees were sharp and poked right into me."[1]

During a guest spot that night, Doug played "Steel Guitar Rag." He also shared the stage with the Hillbilly Shakespeare at the Skyline Club in Austin on December 19, 1952. Two weeks later, Hank would succumb to heart failure caused by a combination of alcohol, morphine, and chloral hydrate.

Doug's paternal grandfather, Alfred Sahm, had emigrated with his family from Germany to central Texas in the early 1900s. Supplementing his cotton and grain farm in the Cibolo area, near San Antonio, Alfred played in a Tex-Mex polka band, the Sahm Boys.

Young Doug's love of conjunto music was encouraged by J. R. Chatwell, a family friend who played fiddle for Czech-German bandleader Adolph Hofner and Tejano musicians on San Antonio's West Side, including tenor saxophonist Rocky Morales and Johnny Perez, a Golden Gloves boxer turned drummer. The boy "wanted to be a Chicano," says Flaco. "Sometimes he'd say, 'I'm not Doug Sahm. I'm Doug Saldaña.'" The Sir Douglas Quintet would release an album called *The Return of Doug Saldaña* in 1971.

Doug played western swing at first, mixing hillbilly string-band music with swinging big-band jazz. The year he was born, Bob Wills & the Texas Playboys released their first record, "San Antonio Rose." Los Texmaniacs recorded it on *Texas Towns & Tex-Mex Sounds.*

Blues and R&B set Doug's passion ablaze. He and a friend, Homer Callahan, spent hours listening to Callahan's stacks of blues 45s. Late at night, Doug would sneak out and walk a couple of hundred feet through the field separating his home and the Eastwood Country Club. He'd spend the rest of the night reveling in the soulful music of T-Bone Walker, Bobby "Blue" Bland, Hank Ballard, Clarence "Gatemouth" Brown, and others.

Becoming a regular at the Tiffany Club, on the West Side, Doug further immersed himself in R&B grooves. He was soon welcomed onstage. By his ninth birthday, he was already playing with Eddie Dugosh & the Ah-Ha Playboys. (Dugosh would switch to rockabilly in 1955.) Bandleader Rudy "Tutti" Grayzell, a regular on *Louisiana Hayride*, sometimes picked Doug up from school. Claiming to be Doug's uncle, he'd arrange to have him dismissed to play with his band, the Cool Cats.

After a brief stint as electric guitarist for blues singer Little Jimmy Jay,

Doug hooked on with Mississippi-born blues guitarist Jimmy Johnson. He was the band's only White member.

Doug formed his own band, the Knights, in 1955. The Mar-kays, the Dell-Kings, the Pharaohs, the Doug Sahm Big Band, and others would follow.

Doug caught the attention of Charles Fitch, owner of a record store and recording studio in Luling, Texas. Fitch boasted of rejecting Willie Nelson's earliest known recording, "When I've Sung My Last Hillbilly Song." Unable to interest Mercury Records in Doug's 1956 demo tape, Fitch released it on his own Sarg Records as Doug's first single, "A Real American Joe" backed with "Rollin' Rollin'," crediting it to Little Doug and the Bandits.

After attending an Elvis Presley concert in San Antonio, Doug was so moved that he added Elvis-like gyrations to his performance during a school talent show. It sparked a riot: the curtains were closed and the show stopped abruptly. Not easily constrained, Doug dropped out of school. He hooked up with tenor saxophonist Vernon "Spot" Barnett. The pair played mostly in Black bars, helping to create the modern South Texas sound.

Doug was fifteen when he met Freddy Fender in 1958. Born Baldemar Garza Huerta on June 4, 1937, Freddy had grown up in the Rio Grande Valley city of San Benito, Texas. His father, a Mexican immigrant, Serapio Huerta, was killed during the last week of World War II in May 1945 and his mother married a migrant farm worker. Working in the fields with his stepfather, young Freddy found escape through music. He debuted on Harlingen, Texas' KGBT at the age of ten, singing "Paloma Querida" by José Alfredo Jiménez Sandoval.

After dropping out of school before his fifteenth birthday, Freddy lied about his age to enlist in the Marines. He would serve three years, spending a considerable amount of that time in the brig, mostly for drinking. Court-martialed in August 1956, he was discharged with the rank of private.

Freddy then returned to Texas and picked up where he had left off. As a rockabilly musician in honky tonks and dance halls, he called himself "El Be Bop Kid." In 1957, after signing with Falcon Records, he released Spanish-language versions of Elvis Presley's "Don't Be Cruel" and Harry Belafonte's "Jamaica Farewell." The latter reached number one on the charts in Mexico and South America. Two years later, Freddy signed with Imperial Records, home of Fats Domino, Ricky Nelson, and Alvin & the Chipmunks. Encouraged by label owner Lew Chudd to change his name, he took "Fender" from the headstock of his guitar, "Freddy" because it sounded good.

Freddy scored a regional hit with "Holy One" in 1959 and recorded "Wasted Days and Wasted Nights" a year later. He had written it in his garage. On the original recording, released by Harlingen, Texas–based Dalton Records, he accompanied himself on guitar. His oldest son, Sonny, played drums. Sonny later drove the Ryder truck carrying the Texas Tornados' equipment.

Freddy had serious problems. He drank whiskey heavily and indulged in "everything from marijuana to cocaine and the needle."[2] In May 1960, he and his bass player were arrested at the border checkpoint in Baton Rouge for possessing the equivalent of two marijuana joints. He told me it was mostly seeds. For what would now be considered a minor offense, he was incarcerated in the Louisiana State Penitentiary—"the Alcatraz of the South." Located on the former Angola plantation, at the end of Route 66, it's approximately twenty-three miles northwest of St. Francisville, Louisiana, and two miles south of Louisiana's border with Mississippi. Set between oxbow lakes on the east side of a bend of the Mississippi River, it's surrounded on three sides by water. It is the United States' largest maximum-security prison, housing 6,300 prisoners as of 2012, 85 percent of whom were listed as violent, and 1,800 staff.[3] *Collier's* magazine called it "the worst prison in America."[4] The laws in 1960 were a lot harsher than they are today.

Through the intervention of then-Louisiana governor Jimmie Davis, composer of "You Are My Sunshine," Freddy received an early release in 1963. Heading to New Orleans, he embraced the city's R&B and Cajun funk and began reviving his career with nightclub gigs. John Broven later wrote in *South to Louisiana: The Music of the Cajun Bayous*, "Although Freddy was a Chicano from Texas marketed as a country artist, much of his formative career was spent in South Louisiana; spiritually Fender's music was from the Louisiana swamps."[5]

In 1968, Freddy returned to Texas and worked full time as a mechanic. He also studied sociology at Del Mar College and played music on the weekends. His first break came when he recorded "Before the Next Teardrop Falls" for Huey Purvis Meaux's Crazy Cajun label in 1974.

Huey was originally a barber, but became a record producer, manager, and promoter. He produced singles for Dale & Grace, Barbara Lynn, Roy Head, Rod Bernard, and Jivin' Gene. The son of poor French-speaking Cajun sharecroppers, he was born in Wright, Louisiana, a small farm town (population 400) seven miles away from Kaplan, near Lafayette. "Back in them days, my

The Texas Tornados, The Hop, Los Angeles, CA

dad worked for the man—picked cotton, hoed, grew rice, shucked it, and harvested it," he told Joe Nick Patoski. "We had four shotgun houses, two black families, two white families. Music was a release. If somebody didn't get cut up and beat the shit out of someone, the dance was considered bad. I was raised that way."[6]

Huey's father, Stanislaus "Pappy Te-Tan" Meaux, played accordion. As a teen, Huey played drums and spoons in his father's trio. They played at house parties where they passed the hat.

Around 1931, Huey and his parents moved to Winnie, Texas, between Houston and Beaumont. After a two-year stint in the US Army, Huey returned to the Lone Star State and enrolled in the Modern Barber College. He opened a barber shop in the early 1950s and supplemented his income by hosting a Friday-night oldies show on KPFT in Houston (where he acquired the title "the Crazy Cajun") as well as hosting teen hops and dances. A local promoter and record producer named Bill Hall shared what he knew about the music business. "That was my college education," Huey Meaux told Petoski. "I didn't think people were supposed to get paid for having fun. Hall would take my records, put his name on them, and take them to the record companies. When we'd go to Nashville, he'd tell me to keep my mouth shut. He said they'd laugh at my accent up there. And I believed him."[7]

The way I heard it, Huey was at a car wash in Corpus Christi when he heard somebody singing nearby. The voice sounded familiar, like Freddy Fender. He walked around the corner and, sure enough, it was Freddy. Huey said, "What are you doing washing cars? Here's my card. You come to Houston, call me."

Freddy followed up a week later, though he was apprehensive about the song Huey wanted him to record. The promoter recalled during an interview with Keith Houk and Paul Schneider that he told Freddy, "'Sing this song, I have to try it.' He said, 'I can't sing that gringo stuff, man.' I said, 'You do it for me or you ain't gonna record no more.' He just wanted to do Mexican songs that everybody had done, and you couldn't sell it for a nickel if you tried. I said, 'Fred, do this thing my way. As long as I'm causing the hits, you just sing your ass off, boy. That's what you got to do.'"[8]

Freddy agreed reluctantly to add his vocals to a prerecorded instrumental track. The song, "Before the Next Teardrop Falls," written by Ben Peters and Vivian Keith, had already been recorded three times, first by Milwaukee-born pop singer Duane Dee in 1968. Before its release, however, Dee was drafted into the Army. His single peaked at number forty-four on the charts. Linda Martell had better luck with the song in 1970, reaching number thirty-three. Jerry Lee Lewis covered it on his 1969 album *Another Time, Another Place*.

Freddy's recording outdid them all. Released nationally by ABC Dot in January 1975, it reached number one on *Billboard*'s pop and country charts, the first time a major-label debut had done so well. "The song makes the singer and the producer," Huey Meaux claimed. "Promotion makes all of it. It's up to the man behind the desk, spending money here and there, taking care of favors, just like you elect a president or governor."[9] His client continued to top the charts with "Secret Love," "You'll Lose a Good Thing," and Spanish-only and bilingual remakes of "Wasted Days and Wasted Nights." *Billboard* named Freddy Fender the Best Male Artist of 1975. Between 1975 and 1983, he charted twenty-one country hits.

Huey Meaux used profits from "Before the Next Teardrop Falls" and the rerecorded "Wasted Days and Wasted Nights" to finance Sugar Hill Recording Studios in Houston and the TNT Records pressing plant in San Antonio. Freddy hated those songs. He told me that it made him sick to his stomach each time he sang them, but he had to do it because they were hits and people wanted to hear them. When he recorded them, Freddy was doing a lot of drugs. He was an alcoholic. He was messed up all the time; he had no idea what was going on business-wise. He was bankrupt and over ten million dollars in debt. Huey Meaux, who was managing him, got him to sign something that he didn't know he was signing. Freddy needed a quick buck, so he signed away his rights to the songs. He never received a cent. It disgusted him to talk about it. You work so hard all your life, and someone comes along and takes advantage of your weaknesses. That's not cool. That's just sharks looking for their dinner—another piece of meat.

"Freddy ripped Freddy off," Augie Meyers claims. "Doug [Sahm] and I had a thing, back in the day, that we called 'MM'—Mexican mentality. Freddy had Mexican mentality. We were in the studio with Huey Meaux after Freddy had the big hit. He got a $600,000 check from ABC Dot. He took the stub off the check, tore it up, and put it in the trash. Huey said, 'Freddy, you'll need that for taxes.' Freddy said, 'They'll never know.' When we started the Texas Tornados, Freddy owed $350,000 to the IRS. Warner Brothers paid it off and Freddy repaid them through our shows."

After recording for Huey's Starlite Records in 1979, Freddy moved to Warner Brothers in 1982. He would score a "Best Latin Pop Album" Grammy for *La Música de Baldemar Huerta* in 2001. Rose Reyes, director of music marketing for the Austin Convention and Visitors Bureau, later said, "When he did Mexican standards at that point in his career, I expected it to be good because he's a perfectionist. But that record is so beautifully recorded; his voice is perfection. I was so proud it was coming back to his roots."[10]

Freddy had a pretty successful movie career. He appeared in *Short Eyes* (1977), the Robert M. Young–directed film adaptation of Miguel Piñero's play; *She Came to the Valley* (1979), co-starring Ronee Blakley, Scott Glenn, and Dean Stockwell; and Robert Redford's *The Milagro Beanfield War* (1998).

Freddy always had his guard up, but, once you got to know him, he was the coolest guy ever. When I met him, he was hard on me. Later, he was under my mom's car fixing it.

Freddy loved Denny's. He used to make our road manager get us rooms at La Quintas. There was always a Denny's next door or close by. Freddy would say, "Let's go eat." I'd say, "Okay, where are we going?" "Denny's." He'd eat there anytime—breakfast, lunch, and dinner. He loved their steak.

One time, Freddy came to San Antonio. He called me when he got in and said, "Let me take you to dinner," so I went over to his hotel. "Okay, Freddy, where do you want to go?" I was sure it was going to be Denny's, but he said, "Let's go to Red Lobster." I asked him why and he went, "I just saw a commercial saying that Red Lobster has delicious, succulent, jumbo shrimp. They sure look good on television."

Freddy was a recovering alcoholic. He checked into a rehab center in 1985 and kept going to AA meetings, even though he hadn't had a drink in years. The Texas Tornados needed two tour buses because Flaco drank and Doug and Augie liked to smoke, as well as pretty much everybody in the band. Freddy, the sound engineer, and some of the road crew traveled in one bus and the rest of us traveled with Doug, Augie, and Flaco. Doug would say, "Okay, all the groovers on my bus and all the non-groovers on Freddy's bus."

We'd sit in the back of the bus, listening to music, smoking, and laughing. Flaco would be drinking beer. They were long bus rides. Occasionally, Freddy would come on Doug's bus, look at us, and say, "You guys are going to hell."

Doug was a real character. When the Texas Tornados played in Hollywood, we would stay at the Garland Hotel. One time, after we arrived, Flaco said to me, "Do me a favor: Get a cart and load my accordion and suitcases." I went to the lobby, grabbed a cart, and pulled it all the way to the bus. I got Flaco's accordion and two big suitcases, and my suitcases and bajo sexto, and loaded everything onto the cart. I went back onto the bus to get Flaco. We talked for a few minutes. "Okay, Flaco, we're ready to go." We walked through the aisles of the bus. When we got off, we saw our luggage on the sidewalk. We saw Doug walking into the hotel with his stuff on the cart.

We recorded *Austin City Limits* in October 1999. A month later, on November 18, Doug died of a heart attack in his sleep. He had celebrated his fifty-eighth birthday two weeks before. He wasn't sick or anything. I remember getting a phone call from Flaco. He said, "We just found out that Doug died." Flaco was quiet. We were both in shock. Then Augie called. I was sitting in my living room, watching television. "Max, bad news, man." "I think I just heard it—is it true?" Augie was crying. He couldn't control himself. "It's true, he's gone." My heart dropped. The whole reason I had moved to Austin was because of Doug. He was constantly telling me, "You've got to move to Austin. It's a groove. The music scene is hot."

"Doug's passing was like losing my right arm," Augie says. "We talked every day. Freddy and I were in Phoenix when we heard. My son called and asked me what I was doing. He had played drums with Doug and me in the Tornados and the Quintet. He has a studio. Doug and I cut an album there, but we never released it. I told him I was in a hotel restaurant, getting ready to eat a sandwich. He asked if I was sitting down. I told him, 'Yes,' and he said, 'Doug just passed away last night. They found his body this morning.' It didn't seem real. I had just talked to him two days earlier. He was in New Mexico. He called me 'Boogie' all the time. He said, 'Boogie, I'm going to go to Taos, find me a couple of acres of land, and build a house. I like that weather.' He was in a hot tub that night with a chick, smoking a joint and drinking Jack Daniels. If you've got high blood pressure, which he did, you don't go in a hot tub or smoke a joint in a high altitude. Around ten o'clock, he called his girlfriend in Austin and told her that he wasn't feeling well. She suggested that he go to the emergency room, but he told her not to worry, that he had vitamins that would take care of it. She said, 'Okay, I'll talk to you later.' She called an hour later and there was no answer. She thought he might have gone to get something to eat or fallen asleep. She called two hours later and there was still no answer. She called the hotel, in the morning, and asked them to check his room. They found him lying on the floor. Freddy and I were going to cancel our show, but we couldn't. Freddy had spent his share of the deposit, so we just went ahead and did the show. As soon as we finished, we flew back home."

We were asked to be pallbearers—Ernie Durawa, Louie Ortega, a couple of the horn players, and me. It was sad. Augie remembers, "It was a big funeral. When we were in the church, the preacher's phone rang in the middle of his sermon. Somebody yelled out, "I think it's Doug calling.'"

Doug experienced a lot in his fifty-eight years. His 1958 single "Crazy Daisy" reached the top twenty in San Antonio. By then, he was playing six nights a week at the Tiffany Lounge for $50 a week. Two years later, "Why, Why, Why" became his first big hit, reaching the top five locally. Setting out in his 1956 Oldsmobile, Doug embarked on a road trip that would include California, Chicago, and New York. That wanderlust would be a constant theme.

After returning to San Antonio in 1961, Doug formed a nine-piece, horn-driven band and topped the charts locally with "Crazy, Crazy Feelin.'" He soon left again for California, scoring an extended gig at a Bakersfield hotel. By the time he returned to Texas, he was married to his first wife, Violet, and had fathered the first of his three children. On the cover of the December 7, 1968, *Rolling Stone*, Doug held his young son Shawn. They updated the photo for the cover of the magazine's July 8, 1971 issue.

Doug tried for the longest time to convince Huey Meaux to record him and his bands. Huey continued to put him off, but he was intrigued by the new world coming to popular music. Holed up in a hotel room with a bottle of Thunderbird wine and the Beatles' up-to-then releases, he drank and listened until he thought he recognized the key to the British group's phenomenal sound. "It was all on the beat," he recalled in 1993, "that was it, same as my daddy's Cajun two-step." Huey called Doug and said, "Come on over, man, I'm drunk but I know what we gotta do. You gotta write some tunes with that beat and grow some hair."[11]

Augie remembers it differently. His band, Danny Ezba & the Goldens, had joined Doug and the Mar-Kays (with Rocky Morales) as opening acts for British Invasion rockers The Dave Clark Five. He recalls, "We played early rock & roll—Elvis Presley, Ricky Nelson—the White boy music. Doug's band played R&B and blues. I always liked the blues, but my band didn't." At the concert, Huey Meaux "saw that Doug and I had long hair and told us, 'Why don't you put an English group together?'"

They did just that. Recruiting bassist Jack Barber, drummer Johnny Perez, and maracas player Leon Beatty, they added the noble prefix "Sir" to Doug's name and formed the Sir Douglas Quintet. Shorn in Beatle haircuts and dressed in hip, Carnaby Street–like garb, they purposely mirrored their British competitors. On *American Bandstand*, Dick Clark asked them, "What part of England are you from?" On *Hullabaloo*, guest host Trini López reminded viewers that, despite appearances, the band came from Texas. "We wanted to be like the Rolling Stones," Doug told *Rolling Stone*, "and carry tons of shit in our suitcases and be heavy, you know, and turn everybody on."[12]

The Sir Douglas Quintet's first single, "She's About a Mover," was a top-thirteen hit. It's Tex-Mex rock & roll—a polka. Los Texmaniacs covered it on our first album, *Tex-Mex Groove*, with Cesar Rosas (Los Lobos) singing. Augie told me he was just doing what the bajo sexto would be doing but doing it on a Vox Continental organ. The Kent, England-based Vox Musical Instrument Company introduced its highly portable keyboard in 1962. Two years later, Augie became the first musician in the United States to own one. It provided the heart of the Sir Douglas Quintet's sound.

Augie Meyers was born on May 31, 1940. One of his legs is shorter than the other and he walks with a limp. "I couldn't walk until I was ten," he says. "I had polio, but I started playing piano. I couldn't use my left hand much. Playing guitar was therapy for me to learn to use my left fingers, getting the chords right." He first met Doug, eighteen months younger, in his mother' grocery store when he was eleven. "I helped carry bags to their car," he remembers, "and I saw his guitar. I told him I played piano and a little guitar. We became friends. He already had a band and was jamming with different people. I didn't start playing music until I was fourteen or fifteen and joined a band. When we weren't playing, I'd go to see him play. When he wasn't playing, he'd come to see me. We sat in with each other. We talked about our dreams and what we wanted to do. They all came true."

Doug frequently bought baseball cards at Augie's mother's grocery. Augie says, "He told me that he needed four or five cards, so we went to the back room where there were boxes of unopened baseball cards. Each box had forty-eight packs of cards. We opened them and put the gum aside. Doug looked at the cards, "Nope, I've got all of those." We put the gum back and licked the wrappers closed until we found the cards he was looking for."[13]

The Sir Douglas Quintet toured the United States, opening for James Brown. They toured Europe with the Rolling Stones and the Beach Boys. Augie recalls, "We played shows with the Monkees and Little Richard. I've got a poster on my wall of the Sir Douglas Quintet playing with the Righteous Brothers, the Newbeats, the Kinks, and the Rolling Stones. The ticket price was $2.50, $3.50 at the door."

It wasn't all good times. "We were in San Francisco in the days of free love and free drugs. We thought that kind of spirit went on all over the United States, but it didn't. When Charlie Manson came on the scene, we had beards and long hair. They wouldn't let us into hotels in New York and Chicago. We had a Black saxophone player in 1965. We couldn't go from San Antonio to Florida on Interstate 10. No one would sell us gas. He couldn't eat in a restaurant or stay in a hotel. Our whole band was either Spanish or Black. We played music together; nobody said anything. The world is changing for the worse."

The Sir Douglas Quintet's second single, "The Rains Came," broke into the US top forty, peaking at number thirty-one, but its title, Augie reports, proved prophetic. "We got busted at the Corpus Christi airport for two joints, and we were facing ten to twenty in the penitentiary. After our probation was over, in 1968, Doug went to California. I had a thirty-six-acre ranch with my ex-wife and my son. I had six horses. Doug lived with me and my family for a while before heading west. I couldn't leave Texas, so I started my own band."

Doug was energized by San Francisco's psychedelic rock music and LSD scene. "Fusing country and rock comes much easier when you're stoned," he told *Rolling Stone*. He formed the Honkey Blues Band with bassist Whitney "Hershey" Freeman, drummer George Rains, and pianist Wayne Talbert. Their 1968 album *Honkey Blues*, released on Mercury, was attributed to the Sir Douglas Quintet + 2.

Augie finally relented to Doug's pleas to join him in California. The Sir Douglas Quintet was reborn. "Doug told me, 'I've got this new song, "Mendocino." Why don't you come out here and we can do it?' So I did."

Released in April 1969 as the title track of the resurrected Sir Douglas Quintet's sophomore album, "Mendocino" reached number twenty-seven on the *Billboard* Hot 100 chart. Augie recalls, "We were on top again, with a major hit record, but all it did was get us out of debt." The bilingual "Nuevo Laredo" came out on *Together after Five* (1970). *The Return of Doug Saldaña* (1971) included a remake of Freddy Fender's "Wasted Days and Wasted Nights."

The Sir Douglas Quintet struggled to recapture their early momentum, but Doug's reputation as a roots-minded visionary continued to build. Returning to Texas in 1971, he set up a base in Austin and helped transform the capital city into the epicenter of the outlaw country music scene. "The outlaw thing happened because of Doug Sahm," Steve Earle told *Pitchfork* in 2018. "[He] told Willie Nelson he should play Armadillo World Headquarters and he told Jerry Wexler [of Atlantic Records], 'If you want progressive country music, you need to sign Willie.'"[14]

Cast as a drug dealer in Kris Kristofferson's 1972 film *Cisco Pike*, Doug recorded a new song, "Michoacán," for the soundtrack, crediting it to Rocky & the Border Kings. He reported cheerfully, "It's a song about dope, the best dope around, but the record company thought it was a song about a state in Mexico."[15]

In 1972, Doug was signed as a soloist to Atlantic Records' new country music division and left the Sir Douglas Quintet. The group recorded a final album, *Future Tense*, with Sonny Farlow replacing him. Augie says that

Atlantic Records producer and co-owner Jerry Wexler "was a good friend of Doug and me. Right before he died in August 2008, he called me. I had a record out, *White Boy*, and he said, 'Man, I like your horn arrangements,' but he could never do anything with Doug. If you go to a record store, where would you find Doug Sahm or the Sir Douglas Quintet—rock & roll, blues, or Americana? The Texas Tornados the same way. Would you file it under country music, Tex-Mex music, or conjunto music? We were so many different things. I'm the same way with my own music. 'Hey Baby (Qué Pasó?)' sold seven and a half million copies and was translated into thirty languages, but my next album was R&B and blues. After that, it was country. I'm getting ready to do a bluegrass album. Why not play it all?"

Kris Kristofferson
and Max Baca

Cindy Cashdollar
and Max Baca

Rosanne Cash and Max Baca

above Tomás Herrera, Max Baca, Jorge Herrera, and Josh Baca

right Joe Ely, unknown, Max Baca, Jimmie Dale Gilmore, and Speedy Sparks

Max Baca and Sean Elliott (San Antonio Spurs)

Taj Mahal and Max Baca

EIGHT

EL ORIGEN
(The Origin)

Long before these talented musicians knew I existed, they were joining in different combinations. "I could feel his soul in everything he did," says Flaco. Doug had a knack for knowing what musicians could do and how to blend them.

For his 1973 Atlantic debut *Doug Sahm and Band*, he assembled a band for the ages. Jack Barber, Atwood Allen, and Augie Meyers came over from the Sir Douglas Quintet, George Rains played drums, Dr. John (Mac Rebennack) played piano, and Kenny Kosek played fiddle. The horn section featured Wayne Jackson and Jack Walrath on trumpet and David "Fathead" Newman (who had played with Ray Charles), Rocky Morales (who had played with Doug in the Mar-Kays), and Martin Fierro on saxophone. David Bromberg played dobro, Andy Statman mandolin, and Charlie Owens pedal steel.

Flaco played accordion. It was his first flight out of San Antonio. "When Doug called," he remembers, "I flew to New York the next day. We got together in the studio like it was a big party. They may have rehearsed before I got there, but it seemed spontaneous."

Bob Dylan, who Doug met through a mutual friend, made a rare guest appearance. Harmonizing with Doug and Atwood Allen on Atwood's "It's Gonna Be Easy," he duetted with Doug on his own "Wallflower." Flaco recalls, "He was laid back, a real mellow guy, humble. I was once on tour with Ry Cooder and Dylan was in another place, playing. We had the day off. I told Ry, 'I'm going to have to try to talk to Dylan.' They let me backstage with a VIP pass. I went to his dressing room. He had security. I told one of them that I wanted to talk to Dylan. I mentioned my name and he let me in. They were ironing his trousers for the show. We're good friends, but being musicians, it's hard to run into each other."

Doug Sahm and Band was released in January 1973. It opens with a cover of Charley Pride's "Is Anybody Goin' to San Antone." It peaked at number 125 on *Billboard*'s Top Albums and Tapes chart.

Flaco's playing on *Doug Sahm and Band* caught the attention of Ry Cooder, who had just released an album of jazz, blues, and roots standards, *Paradise and Lunch* (1974) and was preparing to record *Chicken Skin Music* (1976). When he called, Flaco was ready: "I had come back from my first trip overseas after going to England with Peter Rowan. When we got back, he went off to do something without me. I started playing with anybody, free-lancing." *Chicken Skin Music* was way ahead of its time. In a letter accompanying a cassette that George Harrison sent Elton John, the ex-Beatle wrote, "Here are three songs from *Chicken Skin Music*. They're quite old and I realize not the sort of music you're doing, but I send them for the hell of it so you could really get into the accordion."[1]

Ry got a sound on his bajo sexto that was amazing. He used Flaco on so many songs. They did "Stand by Me" with background singers. It was incredible. According to Flaco, "Ry was spontaneous, the same as Doug. They wanted to record with everybody there, live, no overdubbing. Let's all play."

"That's the best way to record," explains producer Joe Treviño. "Everybody else wants to build it up from a click track. They want to make it perfect. There are new technologies available, but we like to know immediately whether a song works or not. The only way to do that is to put the band in the room and let them thrash it out, get a separation on them, and then let it bleed. There's a liveliness. It introduces the size and depth of the record. It amplifies itself."

Going on to produce movie scores, Ry continued to employ Flaco along the way. On *Cruzando Borders*, Los Texmaniacs covered Ry's song "Across the Borderline" from the 1982 film *The Border*, starring Jack Nicholson and Nick Nolte. John Hiatt wrote it. The lyrics are so heavy. Freddy sang it during the closing credits. That song always gets me where it counts. It has so much truth to it. It's a heartfelt story about Mexicans trying to cross the border to the promised land to work to support their families and escape the hardships in Mexico where there're no jobs and everyone is poor. Why can't they cross this river and work? Things changed when they put up the border, but I know people who have crossed it, risking their lives. They had to walk hundreds of miles through deserts, sometimes without food or water.

Freddy told me that when he recorded the song, he almost passed out. It was like when I first recorded with Flaco. He partied the night before and stayed up. All he could remember was that a buddy had come over and left him an eight-ball of coke and a bottle of tequila. He did it all and, all of a sudden, it was time for him to sing. He sang without a single flaw. There's no way I could do that.

Doug followed *Doug Sahm and Band* with *Texas Tornado* (1973), with a slightly altered band. The title tune, written by Doug, featured legendary Chicago blues keyboards player Barry Goldberg. On his next album, *Groover's Paradise* (1974), credited to the Tex-Mex Band, Doug joined with Creedence Clearwater Revival's rhythm section—bassist Stu Cook and drummer Doug Clifford—and Cajun accordionist Link Davis Jr.

Texas Rock for Country Rollers (1976) reunited Doug with Huey Meaux. Huey had spent three years (1969–1972) in prison for transporting an underage female across state lines to a disc jockey convention in Nashville, thereby violating the Mann Act. President Jimmy Carter pardoned him in 1977. Attributed to Sir Doug & the Texas Tornados, *Texas Rock for Country Rollers* came out on ABC Dot and featured Augie, Jack Barber, Atwood Allen, George Rains, and newcomer Harry Hess (steel guitar). Standout tracks included Doug's "Cowboy Peyton Place" and "You Can't Hide a Redneck (Under That Hippy Hair)." Uncle Tupelo would cover "Give Back the Key to My Heart," with Doug singing on their 1993 recording.

After signing with Clifford Antone's blues label in 1979, Doug dedicated the horn-driven *Hell of a Spell* to Mississippi-born guitarist Guitar Slim (Eddie Jones) (1926–1959). Doug and Augie reunited on *Still Growing* (1982), on the UK Sonet label, credited to "Augie Meyers with Doug Sahm." *The "West Side" Sound Rolls Again* came out the next year, credited to Doug Sahm, Augie Meyers, and the West Side Horns.

Other than scoring a crossover hit with Rockin' Sidney's "Don't Mess with My Toot Toot" in 1985, Huey Meaux turned from producing and artist management to song publishing. His empire crumbled, however, when a dispute with his adopted son resulted in the police raiding his home and discovering thousands of photographs and videos of mostly underaged females. Huey was arrested for possession of child pornography. The charges increased after his live-in girlfriend's daughter filed a $10 million civil suit claiming he had been molesting her for sixteen years, beginning when she was nine. Huey pleaded guilty to two counts of sexual assault of a child, along with a drug possession charge and a child pornography charge. Charges were added for jumping bail and fleeing briefly to Juárez, Mexico. He was sentenced to fifteen years in prison. Released in 2007, he succumbed to multiple organ failure four years later.

Following an automobile accident in 1986, Doug headed north to Vancouver, Canada. There, he hooked up with pianist Gene Taylor and guitarist Amos Garrett and recorded *The Return of the Formerly Brothers* for Alberta-based Stony Plain Records, whose product was distributed by Warner Brothers. The concert album *Live in Japan, 1990* was released a year after it was recorded.

Doug and Augie had a tremendous following in Europe, especially in the Scandinavian countries. "Meet Me in Stockholm," from the Sir Douglas Quintet's 1987 *Midnight Sun* album, went platinum and was one of the year's best-selling records in Denmark, Norway, and Sweden.

In the mid-1980s, Doug agreed to perform at a friend's wedding in Austin and needed musicians. He phoned bassist Speedy Sparks, who suggested John X. Reed, a New Mexico–born guitarist raised in Lubbock, and drummer Frosty Smith. Alvin Crow from Oklahoma City joined in on fiddle and vocals. Excited about the band, Speedy (who owned a local label, Dynamic Records) contacted Paris-based New Rose Records. The French label was eager to sign the group. Covering rock & roll classics by Buddy Holly, Chuck Berry, the Rolling Stones, and Van Morrison, Doug and the Texas Mavericks recorded what would be their only studio album, *Who Are These Masked Men?*, in a quick three days. Taking the album's title seriously, the band wore masks on stage and adopted aliases. A show during their tour of Germany, with Mike Buck replacing Smith, was broadcast by Radio Bremen. The recordings were presumed lost for nearly four decades, but *Live in Bremen, 1987* was eventually released in 2017.

On returning to Texas in 1988, Doug reconnected with Clifford Antone, joining Angela Strehli and Flaco in Antone's Texas R&B Revue. *Juke Box Music*, comprising R&B and doo-wop covers, came out on Antone's in 1990. *The Last Real Texas Blues Band featuring Doug Sahm* (1994) included the Whole

Wheat Horns, drummer George Rains, guitarists Denny Freeman and Derek O'Brien, and saxophonist Rocky Morales. Half of the album was recorded at Antone's. The complete show would be released in 2012 as *Live in Stockholm*.

Doug Sahm's dreams of a Tex-Mex version of the Traveling Wilburys, the supergroup featuring Bob Dylan, George Harrison, Roy Orbison, Tom Petty, and Jeff Lynne, turned into the Texas Tornados in 1989. "I had a record—'Hey Baby (Qué Pasó?)'—on Atlantic," remembers Augie. "They weren't doing anything with it, so I returned their money and bought my contract back. Doug called me a little later and asked if I was planning to go with another label. I told him, 'No, I'm going to start my own label.' Then he said, 'Warner Brothers wants us to put together a super Tex-Mex group.' I said, 'Who do you got in mind?' 'I'm going to get Flaco Jiménez.' 'Who else?' 'Johnny Rodríguez or Freddy Fender?' I said, 'Get Freddy Fender.'"

Six years later, I joined. By then, they were a well-established powerhouse. It was a wonderful opportunity to play great music.

NINE

EL MOVIMIENTO

(Moving)

When I started with the Texas Tornados, I'd come home from a tour and play with my brother. That went on until 1997 when I decided to move to Austin. Doug had been telling me to move there, saying, "It's a really hip town, plus you'll save on airfare."

At the time, I was heartbroken. That gave me more of a reason to get out of Albuquerque. I had lived with a woman for three years, the love of my life. She had a nine-to-five job at a trucking company. She was from California. I met her on the road. I had just bought my recording studio. I set it up in the strip mall where my dad had his tax office. I invested money and bought recording gear. We built a control booth and a vocal booth.

Everyone has problems, of course, but she knew I was a musician when we met. For whatever reason, she wanted a different life. She started thinking that she was going to be stuck in Albuquerque. We talked about someday moving to Texas together, but once I had my studio, I had more reason to stay. I guess she thought she could move on without me.

One day, I got the biggest shock of my life. I had been recording. She called around five in the evening, after she got out of work. We didn't have cell phones. I answered the call in the studio office. She said, "What time are you coming home for dinner?"

I said, "I'm going to have to pass. I'm working on a project. I have a band coming in and I'm going to be working with them until ten."

She said, "Okay, I'll make dinner. It'll be in the oven when you get home."

That was it, the last thing she ever told me. When it came time, I closed the studio and drove home. When I got there, I didn't realize that her car was gone. The lights were off. I just parked where I usually parked. I opened the door to the house and paused. "Wait a minute."

We had two chihuahua dogs who would usually greet me, but there was no barking. I turned the light on and the whole house was empty. There was nothing in the living room—no furniture, nothing. She hadn't taken the stove or refrigerator, but there was no kitchen table or chairs. In the bedroom—nothing. She left one box with my clothes and a picture of me and her on top. She didn't even leave a note. The first thing I thought was "We've been robbed."

It was a shock to the brain and to the heart. I didn't know what was going on. I couldn't digest it. I called my older sister and she came over with my mom. When they walked in, they started freaking out, too. I was in shock; I couldn't say anything. My sister said, "You've got to accept the fact that she's left you."

It was hard. Where could I sleep? She had taken the bed. I stayed at my mom's, but I was so much in shock. I felt humiliated and betrayed: so many mixed emotions going through me. I didn't have a clue where she was going. I couldn't stay in that house anymore. My dad felt my pain. He said, "C'mon, son, get a bag."

My aunt and her husband owned a ranch in the mountains south of Albuquerque. My dad and my brother and I used to go deer hunting there. This time, my dad and I stayed four or five days. He wanted me to clear my mind. There were no phones or internet. I'm so grateful he did that. If I had stayed in Albuquerque, I would have gotten in my truck and gone to look for her, but I didn't know where to look. I called her boss, but she instructed everybody at work to not tell me anything.

"He never let us know," my mom says. "He went through what he went through by himself. As far as we were concerned, he was fine. He never let us know how depressed or sad he was, but as a mother, there were times I would feel a heavy heart."

When I got back from the mountains, I had a clearer mind. That's when I made the decision to move. I couldn't stay there anymore. Her leaving had something to do with it, but it was the beginning of a new life. I packed my clothes, my bajo sexto, and eighty dollars—all the money I had to my life. She had cleared out our bank account. I didn't have furniture, but I had a full tank of gas.

I told my brother, "Come to Austin and we'll put the band together. There's a better opportunity for us here, more exposure for this kind of music."

My mom says, "Donny kept telling him to come to Texas, but Jimmy had kids and wasn't keen on moving out of New Mexico." Jimmy stayed in Albuquerque: "I didn't want to leave Josh's mother. In the music business, you've got to be gone for a long time sometimes. I didn't want to leave her. She didn't want to go to Texas. How stupid I was. If I had known in the long run, we'd break up anyway, I would have gone."

"My husband was very upset," says my mom. "He'd say, 'He's leaving his brother hanging. He's going to go to starve. Where's he going to play? It's hard to break into the Tejano scene.'"

I asked my mother, "What's the worst thing that could happen? If I don't make it, I'll come home." She remembers that she told me "to go and give it his best. He left with his truck, two hundred dollars in his pocket, and his bajo sexto, and never moved back. When my husband saw how good he was doing, he was proud and happy."

"It hurt when Los Hermanos Baca broke up," says Josh. "They had a really good thing going. I watched them my entire life. They were incredible. They created chemistry. Being brothers, they fought, but my dad, being the dominant brother, was hard-headed."

Jimmy hasn't been gigging or jamming much. Josh explains, "He hurt his back and started taking pain killers. It brought him down a hard road but he's doing much better. He calls every day and asks me how the kids are doing. That's one thing I give him; I respect that. He was there for me as a kid but not really there. His mind was always somewhere else. I was raised by my grandmother and Aunt Maxine. I started playing music to make money. I didn't want to be the black sheep of the family. I came at the time when the high life started dying out. My grandpa passed away. My grandma couldn't work much. Everything changed. I had to be on my own, as much as I could, but my family was always there, no matter what."

I stayed with a friend in Austin for a few weeks and then found an apartment for $600 a month. I drove back and forth between there and San Antonio, going to recording studios to work.

4 Aces was the Texas Tornados' fourth album for Warner Brothers. We still had one to do. By that time, they had been touring for seven or eight years.

Doug and Freddy were always bickering, a real power struggle. It would get pretty steamy sometimes. They never got into fist-fights, but they were constantly disagreeing, always butting heads. There were times I thought they were going to come to blows. Flaco and Augie stayed quiet. They wouldn't get involved in the argument. It would go on until we got on stage. The road manager would come over to them and say, "Knock it off!" They'd do a hell of a show.

"I got along with everybody," says Flaco. "Freddy and Doug—uh, uh, uh. Disagreements. Sometimes there would be meetings. Freddy, Doug, and Augie would be there, but I wasn't. I never went to meetings. I knew in the long run that it would be okay. In any job, there are contradictions. I don't like to argue. I get nervous so I just laid back. I had a right to say something, but I didn't want to stir the water. I could hear them discussing finances, the gigs, this and that, in a hotel room. I just passed them by. I walked the aisle and that was it. I didn't want any part of it."

Freddy was used to performing *The Freddy Fender Show* in casinos in Las Vegas, Reno, and Atlantic City. He was a country music superstar. I saw him for the first time at the New Mexico State Fair. He wanted his band to replace the Texas Tornados band. That's where the trouble started. He wanted his own drummer, his guitar player (Charlie Rich's son Allen), and his bass player, but Doug said, "No."

When the Texas Tornados started, they made money big-time, but after a good six- or seven-year run, the money wasn't there anymore. They went from $100,000 a show to $30,000 a show. Thirty thousand may sound like a lot, but, with four principal guys, four musicians in the band, the road crew, trucks, flights, and hotels, it didn't go a long way. We recorded *Live from the Limo* at Antone's and completed the record deal. That was pretty much it.

The Texas Tornados used to tour from April to June and then take a break. Doug and Augie would go out with Doug's sons, Shawn and Shandon, as the Sir Douglas Quintet. Doug also played shows with Alvin Crow as The Mysterious Sam Dogg and the Cosmic Cowboys, wearing wrestling masks during performances.

Augie says, "Doug liked doing different things, even when we were in the Texas Tornados. We were on top, a supergroup, making big time money, but he'd say, 'I'm going to take a break and go play jazz.' Freddy Fender would say,

'You don't know how to play jazz,' but he was wrong. Doug knew jazz and he'd go off to play it." "We had different things going on," explains Flaco. "I had my own band. Doug, Augie, and Freddy had their own gigs."

During breaks, Flaco and I would go to Europe, where he had an incredible following. At first, I mostly played bass. Óscar Téllez played bajo sexto. We'd switch off. The first time overseas with Flaco, we toured Spain. I had to get a passport. We were in our second week of the tour. We were having fun, but we weren't used to the food. It was different from what we had in New Mexico. After a while, we just wanted a tortilla, beans, chili, enchiladas. We went to a restaurant. We were reading the menu when David, Flaco's son, said, "Hey man, look, they have tortillas. Oh, my God, I would die for a tortilla."

The waiter came and I said, "Let me have a bowl of alubias (beans) and a tortilla. As a matter of fact, give me two tortillas." David said, "I'll take the same thing." Flaco said, "That sounds great." Óscar said, "Me, too."

We didn't know that tortillas in Spain are not flour tortillas. They're potato and egg omelets, the size of a pie. We had ordered two each. We took them with us and ate them the rest of the tour.

One time, Flaco punched the monitor guy and knocked him out. We were doing Michael Martin Murphey's Wild West Fest in Santa Fe. Flaco had just signed with Arista Records out of Nashville. The record label people were there. The governor was in the crowd. There were ten thousand people on this field. It was a big deal.

We got on stage and started playing. Flaco couldn't hear his accordion. I turned to the monitor guy and asked him to pick up the level of Flaco's accordion. He picked up the volume and it started feeding back and screeching. He turned it down and Flaco looked at me again: "I need more accordion. I can't hear myself."

The monitor guy turned the system up again and it squealed. He had an attitude. He was one of those sound engineers who thought we worked for him instead of him accommodating us. He obviously didn't know about frequencies. The audience was having trouble with the sound; it was distracting from the show. Then the guy turned the monitors completely off and crossed his arms, like, "Okay, what are you going to do now?" We had to play the rest of the show—four more songs—without monitors. We finished as best as we could. Flaco broke reeds on his accordion, he had to play so hard. When we were done, Flaco said, "Ladies and gentlemen, thank you. I'm Flaco Jiménez.

This is my band. Let's give a round of applause for that soundman in the house. He did a fantastic job—but the guy running the monitors sucks!"

The crowd went crazy. It pissed the monitor guy off. You could see it in his face. Flaco started walking off the stage. I was right behind him. Flaco was getting to the stairs when the monitor guy charged him. Boom! Flaco landed a right jab across his jaw. The guy dropped like a sack of potatoes. He was out like a light. Security came. They were going to take Flaco to jail. Backstage, there were lots of press people and people from the record label. I yanked Flaco's arm and said, "Let's go." I put him in my van, gathered the rest of the band, and we took off. We got out of there as quick as we could. I had never before seen Flaco hit anyone. He always maintained his cool, but the guy was charging at him. He didn't have a choice; he was protecting himself. Skinny Flaco has a mighty right punch.

Flaco and I were on a bus once, driving to California. We were sitting in the front, watching the road and reading signs. There was a sign that said, "Portola Avenue." I said, "That's a weird name for a street." Flaco said, "It sounds like some kind of Mexican food."

We started laughing. Flaco said, "Let's go to a restaurant and order a bowl of portola."

Sure enough, we stopped at a Mexican restaurant to have lunch. Everybody ordered—Doug, Freddy, Augie, the band. It was Flaco's turn. He was looking at his menu. In Spanish, he told the waitress, "Let me have a bowl of portola."

She began writing it down, but stopped, looked at him, and said, "What?"

Flaco said, "We're from Texas. We've come all the way here because they recommended this restaurant for the best portola."

The waitress looked at the menu and said, "I don't see it. I've just started working here, but I don't know what that is."

Flaco tried explaining it to her, "You get a tortilla, a portola, cheese, and onions and roll them together."

"Do you mean a burrito?"

"No, no, a portola."

The waitress went to ask the cook. We were all laughing by this time. We could see her talking to the cook. He shook his head, waved his hands, and said something to her. She came back to our table and told Flaco, "Sir, I talked to the cook and he said, 'We have it only on Tuesdays.'"

It was hilarious. Flaco is such a character. One time, we were on stage with the Texas Tornados. There were twelve thousand people in the audience. Doug started introducing the musicians in the band. "Ladies and gentlemen, this is Augie Meyers." Everyone started going crazy. "This is Ernie Durawa: he's single if any of you women aren't taken. This is Freddy Fender. He's married so he can't mess around. This is Max Baca. He's single so he can mess around." Flaco gets on the mic and goes, "Hi, I'm Flaco. I'm married, but I mess around."

Flaco loves playing with other musicians, though he's incredibly humble. He recorded a Chuck Berry tune, "Havana Moon," with Willie Nelson and Carlos Santana in 1983. It turned out to be the title track of Santana's solo album. Flaco remembers, "It was a very laid-back session."

TEN

ESTIRÁNDOSE
(Stretching)

In early 1994, Flaco and I were touring, just the two of us. We flew to Los Angeles to do shows with the Rock Angels, Louie Mendez's and Lorenzo Martínez's band, who, says Lorenzo, "were from East L.A. and played a mix of Tex-Mex, Cajun, and blues."

The Rock Angels sang in English and Spanish but had a zydeco sound with a rub-board player and an accordion. I dug what they did. They opened for the Texas Tornados. We met backstage and remained good friends. Through the years, we kept in touch. Lorenzo would come to Albuquerque, where I had my recording studio. I invited him to come and record some tunes. He recorded three or four with my brother and me. They were never released.

Lorenzo was born in Los Angeles and started out playing big band music. "I did some Tex-Mex," he says, "but it was orchestral style. I was lucky enough to be brought up in the area of Norwalk. There was a band there, Banda Brava. They had Texas roots, but they also played salsa music. I enjoyed hanging out with them. Their saxophone player showed me how to play." In addition to drums and saxophone, Lorenzo plays bass, guitarrón, and vihuela. He's a great singer. He "played mariachi music at UCLA. I was one of the first in their mariachi program, but I didn't complete it. We were on the road, making money."

Lorenzo says, "Mariachi comes from southern-to-mid Mexico. They played with violins and harp. It wasn't always the guitarrón. The bass notes were played by the harp. Different regional styles developed. South Americans have the armadillo charango. The Mexicans got the idea of the tortoise shell for the impregnated back of the guitarrón. It's not flat; it's rounded. So is the vihuela, a smaller, percussive, stringed instrument. All stringed instruments trace back to Spain but those two—guitarrón and vihuela—developed in Mexico."

Lorenzo played drums out of necessity: "I used to see bands needing a strong, confident backbeat. They thought they were grooving, but they weren't. I thank the Lord I could feel timing, whether it's a little bit off or not. I could make things happen with the drums. It makes the band more relaxed and sounding better. It's more danceable. Because I play other instruments, I understand the placement of a beat or a chord, what's needed and what's not needed. My approach has always been simplicity. I grew up listening to a group that played simply—Los Alegres de Terán. They were all about the vocals. The musicians supported the vocals. I've always loved that. It's so important to have a proper rhythm section."

The Rock Angels' manager called Flaco and me and asked if we'd be interested in touring with them, a two-week run. "It was a meeting of different regional styles," remembers Lorenzo: "Chicano and Tejano, but there was common ground. Flaco enjoyed my singing of traditional ballads. Max backed me up. It was a lot of fun. There was a whole lot of sharing. It was like we knew each other forever. That's what music does; it brings everyone together."

The first night of the tour, we played Luna Park. We were hanging out backstage, while the opening band was playing, when we got a message telling us to call this number as soon as possible and speak to Don Was. I went to a pay phone and called. I wasn't familiar with Don Was, but he told me that he was producing an album (*Voodoo Lounge*) for the Rolling Stones in Hollywood. He had seen in the newspaper that Flaco was performing at Luna Park. "Yes sir, he's right here."

"Would you ask him if he'd be interested in recording on a track? We're going to be in the studio tomorrow." As Don Was explained it, he and the Rolling Stones had gotten stuck on a song—"Sweethearts Together." They had tried using steel guitar, piano, and saxophone to get a Tex-Mex sound, but nothing worked. That's why he called Flaco.

Flaco got on the phone and said, "Sure I could do the song. What key is it in?" Afterward, he turned to me and asked, "Who's the Rolling Stones?"

"I was into country music," Flaco explains. "The roots—Bob Wills, Tex Ritter. My favorite instrument was the pedal steel." That's where Flaco gets his unique sound. He still thinks like a steel guitar player. He doesn't overdo it, just adds those beautiful melodic crescendos. He makes the accordion cry, but he gets his ideas from how the pedal steel sneaks in. Flaco never steps on the one who's singing, but compliments what they're singing.

Flaco asked for a cassette of the Rolling Stones' song. There were no CDs or mp3s yet. After we finished doing the show and got back to the hotel, there was a tape waiting. Flaco listened to it and said, "This should be easy."

The song was similar to a bolero—a slow rock ballad. Flaco knew what he was going to do on the accordion, but he asked me, "What rhythm are you going to play?" I told him I could give it a Tex-Mex feel, a fast bolero strum. It fit right in. Flaco called Don Was, who told him the Rolling Stones had been trying for a Tex-Mex sound. Flaco said, "I could do it, no problem," and he said, "I have my bajo sexto player with me, the partner of the accordion." "Bring him too, we want him."

The next day, we took a cab to the studio. "We didn't have a lot of time," recalls Flaco. "We had to fly to San Francisco for a show before going home."

I was freaking out; I didn't know what to expect. I'd heard stories about the Rolling Stones' wild parties. As we were walking into A&M Studios, Charlie Watts and Ron Wood and their wives came out of the control room and greeted us: "How're you doing, Flaco? How're you doing, Max?" We shook their hands and walked into the control room. Ron Wood was sitting with Mick Jagger and studio engineer Don Bosworth. Jagger got up and welcomed us. Flaco remembers, "Jagger handed me a Miller Lite. I'm not a heavy beer drinker, but it was a present."

Microphones were already set up for Flaco and me. When I took my bajo sexto out, Keith Richards saw it from a distance. He was sitting in a corner, smoking a cigarette. He got up and walked over. He pointed to my bajo sexto and asked, "What's that?" I told him it was a bajo sexto and he asked if he could see it. He really examined it, turning it upside down and around, while chuckling in this raspy voice. He tried playing it like a guitar, but I explained that it was tuned in fourths, not fifths. He managed to get a I chord, and I showed him a V chord. By that time, his cigarette had burnt to the end. An ash fell on my bajo sexto, the cherry part of the sugar. He went, "I'm sorry," and tried wiping it off with his hand. It still has that burn mark on it.

He was amazed by my bajo sexto and said, "This is so cool. Will you sell it to me?" It totally caught me off guard. I looked over at Flaco and he just shrugged his shoulders. "Man, Mr. Richards, I don't know. My dad gave me this. It's got sentimental value." "Name your price." I was thinking maybe twenty thousand, a hundred thousand. I didn't know. He looked at me again and repeated "Name your price." He told me three times, but I couldn't do it to my dad. I said, "Mr. Richards, I don't think I could sell it." "You sure? Name your price"

I didn't sell it, but I wrote the number down to Macias' workshop in San Antonio and gave it to him. He wanted that bajo sexto right there and then and was willing to pay whatever I might sell it for. When we finished the tour and I got back home to Albuquerque, I told my dad about it. He said, "Pendejo! You could have bought the whole factory!"

Flaco remembers, "I didn't know the song, and I didn't know what to expect. Don Was came over the intercom and said, 'We're going to play it once so you can get acquainted with it.' They played a recording of the song. It came to my mind that I could play around with it. It was so simple."

Flaco and I tried a run-through and then saddled up for the recording. Flaco said, "I think we're ready." Don Was got on the intercom and said, "No, we've got you already." They had recorded us while we were rehearsing and setting the levels. They rolled the tape without telling us. How it came out is how it came out. It was a brilliant trick. If I had done it again, I might have started over-thinking about what I could do. It might have become mechanical. This way, we were loose and free. We blended right in. We weren't worried that the red light was on. I played what I felt, Flaco played what he felt, and it worked. Flaco says of that session, "I was happy with it. I know it's there. We didn't have to overdub, nothing. It was a keeper."

Some time later, the Rolling Stones' attorney called me and said, "I want to make sure we credit the banjo [sic] sexto player."

When the album came out and I saw my name in the credits, it finally hit me—I'd recorded with the Rolling Stones! At the session, my adrenaline had been too pumped up and I had been too starstruck to think about it.

Three months after the recording session, the Rolling Stones sent me a double-platinum disc marking more than two million sales. I hung it on my wall. That's how many people buy Rolling Stones albums. The manufacturers couldn't print them fast enough. You've got to give them credit.

Our relationship with Lorenzo Martínez continued to grow. He says today

Flaco Jiménez, Keith Richards, Max Baca, Mick Jagger

from his Los Angeles home, "I started working with Flaco and Max more extensively, playing drums. They'd come to town to play at the Taste of Texas. Nick Martínez, who's no longer with us, owned it. It was where all the Tex-Mex conjuntos performed. It was a beautiful time."

The conjunto scene in Los Angeles differs from the conjunto scene in Texas. "L.A. is a mecca for so many different styles," says Lorenzo, "not only Latin American, but we also have the Arabic style, the European style, and even the Cuban style. The Cuban Son (which originated in the late nineteenth century and blends Cuban, African, and Indigenous elements) is a big influence. It's been booming from the mid-'90s to today, but we've always kept our Mexican American roots."

Lorenzo played with the "father of Chicano music," Eduardo "Lalo" Guerrero (1916–2005), the great Tucson-born guitarist/vocalist/farm labor activist. "Lalo was an eighty-five-year-old teenager," Lorenzo recalls. "He loved to have fun and create music on the spot, on stage. He was very comical and wrote a lot of parodies. 'People are too serious,' he'd say, and he'd lighten up the audience. We toured with Flaco and Max in Paris, France. There was a beautiful connection."

ELEVEN

EMPUJANDO HACIA ADELANTE
(Pushing Forward)

Flaco had a big hit in 1995 as a featured guest on the Mavericks' "All You Ever Do Is Bring Me Down." "He played a solo," says Josh, "and it was so cool that an accordion could do that. My dad and my uncle were playing in bars—four- or five-hour gigs. They started covering it."

Growing up, Josh listened to rock, blues, country, hip-hop, and conjunto music, but when he woke in the morning, he would immediately listen to Flaco. He recalls, "My dad would say, 'Put on some Mingo Saldivar,' and that would be great, too. When I turned eight or nine years old, my grandmother took me to the Tejano Conjunto Festival. It was the first time that I got to experience Texas conjunto music, the vibes, the culture, the energy that Texas brings to this music. The roots grew there. I could feel the vibe. That night, there was a band with bad-ass musicians. They were jumping around and dancing. There was more than what I had been doing back home. I wanted to do this."

The last two acts of the night were Mingo Saldivar and Flaco Jiménez: "Mingo did 'Ring of Fire" and 'Folsom Prison Blues,' all these Johnny Cash songs my Uncle Carl played when I hung out with him, but he was playing them on accordion and singing them in Spanish. My Uncle Donny was up there, playing bajo sexto with Óscar Téllez. They were jamming. It was cool. I was just standing there when suddenly, I heard Mingo say, 'I want to invite a good friend who's come all the way from Albuquerque, New Mexico to come up and play—Josh Baca.'"

Then it was Flaco's turn: "Flaco got on stage and wailed. Flaco being Flaco said, 'I want to invite a good friend of mine and he is one of the best, if not the best, accordion player and singer I've ever heard. I want to invite Esteban Jordan to play a song with me.' Wow! Flaco and Esteban Jordan singing harmony and playing accordions with me. I couldn't believe it. I'm getting chills just remembering it. My grandpa was there. That was the start of my music. I'm glad he was there. He started it by bringing the accordion back from Germany. He taught my dad and my uncle."

Josh Baca

We recorded *Flaco Jiménez* (1995) at Blue Cat Studios. "It was a very important album," says Joe Treviño, "and it won the Grammy as the year's Best Mexican-American/Tejano Music Performance. It was a stylistic shift for Flaco from a compact, real dry sound to a more airy sound. We brought rock elements into their scene. It crossed over very nicely."

Joe and I met when I was playing with the Texas Tornados in the early 1990s. "We hit it off right off the bat," he remembers. "He's a monster musician, I could tell that immediately. He's a good engineer, too. He's got really good ears. He sometimes catches things that I miss. It's like having a second producer, a best friend who's got your back. His right hand always knows what's going on. I can cover most sessions with Max playing bajo sexto, bass, and drums. The snare drum hits where the bajo sexto hits. He knows exactly where he wants to lay that in. It's seamless. He locks in with anybody. He's such a great musician. It's a pleasure to work with him."

Joe initially produced blues, R&B, and rock records. As he tells it, "Tejano and conjunto music fell into my lap. The first crossover record we did was Flaco's *Flaco Jiménez*. Arista Records had just formed a Latin division. They were going to record Flaco at a friend of mine's studio, but they didn't think it was up to the snuff of the producer, Bill Halverson. They brought him around to our place. He said, 'We could make a record here.' One thing led to another. After working with Flaco, we recorded a bunch of local hits for regional records. San Antonio is like Nashville. There are all kinds of music—blues, jazz, rock—but if you're not cutting country music, you're not really doing anything. Here [Austin], it's all about Tejano and conjunto music. We became established in that genre and got good at it. Thirty-five years later, we're still in the game."

Recording conjunto music is different from recording other music. "It's played by midrange instruments: the accordion and bajo sexto, and it's got a different bottom than blues or rock," Joe explains. "Stylistically, it's night and day, but music is music. At the end of the day, it has to feel right."

Flaco's son, David, played drums. Óscar Téllez and I switched between bajo sexto and bass. He was such a good musician. He could play bass, drums, and accordion and sing. He was just an all-around cat.

The recording session was on a Sunday. We had played with Flaco on Friday and Saturday night. Back in those days, when I was younger, I liked to party—drinking and getting high. Flaco told us to go home after the gig and get some sleep. We had to be at the studio at ten o'clock in the morning. It was a big deal, a major record label out of Nashville. David and I figured we'd go to bed when we went to bed and it'd be fine. We stayed up drinking and having a good time until the wee hours of the morning. It was eight o'clock by the time we went to sleep. I was staying at Flaco's house. It wasn't even nine o'clock yet when Flaco started telling us, "Get up, let's go!"

I felt wounded, hungover, and deprived of sleep. When we got to the studio, they were still setting up the microphones. There was a sofa. As soon as I saw it, I lay down and fell asleep. I slept for maybe twenty minutes before Flaco said, "C'mon, get in there."

I woke from a sound sleep, walked into the recording booth, and strapped on my bass. David counted out the song and we recorded "Open Up Your Heart." It was one take. Flaco never did overdubs; it was all live. He recorded the old-school way, with the whole band playing together. It made it fun and spontaneous. We never rehearsed, just played like we were playing at a dance.

We recorded a few songs. Then somebody made a run to the store and brought back beer. The only way I was going to get through that recording session was to get back on the saddle, so I popped open a beer and drank it. I was back to square one and we were able to finish the album.

I came up with the title of the closing track, "Catwalk." We recorded it in Nashville with slide guitarist Lee Roy Parnell. He walked into the studio, said hello to Flaco, and asked what song they were going to do. Flaco said, "Shit, I don't know."

They strapped on their guitars. All of the musicians were ready to go. Lee Roy said, "How about a blues tune?" Flaco said, "Okay" and started to play. They got through it and everyone in the studio gave each other high fives.

Lee Roy said, "Wow, I've never played that song in my life." He didn't have a name for it, so Flaco asked me, "What do you think we should name this song?" It reminded me of a cat walking through an alley, so I said, "How about 'Catwalk?'" It was perfect.

Flaco Jiménez won a "Best Mexican American Album" Grammy and we went to the awards ceremony. It was awesome. Flaco went up to the podium to receive his award. It was his second Grammy. He was so cool. He thanked his musicians and all his fans. He was very humble, genuine.

We did *Buena Suerte, Señorita* (1996) in ZZ Top's recording studio, the Boiler Room, in Austin. It had gold and platinum albums on the wall. You took an elevator down to the studio. They had the drums already set up: an old five-piece kit. I played bajo sexto and bass, switching off with Óscar Téllez.

Cesar Rosas of Los Lobos and Max Baca

I had learned my lesson. I didn't stay up partying the night before.

Flaco's next album, *Said and Done*, won a Grammy for "Best Tejano Album" of 1998. We recorded it in San Antonio. I played bajo sexto and bass. It was Flaco's third Grammy.

Then came *Sleepytown*, Flaco's first album after Doug's death. Half of it was produced by the Morales brothers, Michael and Ron, and the other half was produced by Dwight Yoakam's guitarist/producer, Pete Anderson. It's got some really cool stuff, like the Beatles' "Love Me Do" with Buck Owens singing, and "Alright, I'm Wrong," with Dwight Yoakam.

In 1999, the year Doug died; Flaco and I did the Los Super Seven project. The Texas Tornados were taking a break. I got a call from Freddy saying,

"Max, we have an offer from RCA Records. They want a super Mexican group." Los Super Seven grew out of a showcase organized by Rick Trevino's manager at the time, Dan Goodman, and publicist Paula Batson, to celebrate Mexican roots music. They did it at a restaurant on South Congress Avenue in downtown Austin during the 1997 South by Southwest. As Rick says, "It was just an event for the press, private. Doug Sahm and Augie Meyers were there, Joe Ely, Rosie Flores, Ruben Ramos, and me. It was a big jam session, just thrown together, but a lot of fun. Afterwards, everybody talked about making a recording. Dan and Paula put their heads together and started figuring out who would want to be part of it. It turned out to be Joe Ely, David Hidalgo and Cesar Rosas of Los Lobos, Ruben Ramos, Freddy Fender, Flaco Jiménez, Max Baca, and me. I recommended that Joel José Guzman be part of the project; he's a great accordion player.

I had been playing with Joel in a local band, the Aztecs, when I went to meet with Steve Berlin, who was producing Los Super Seven's first album. Born in Philadelphia in 1955, Steve had been playing saxophone and producing Los Lobos since 1984. He first heard them when they opened for the Blasters, the Downey, California–based rock band he shared with Dave and Phil Alvin. "I was in the right place at the right time," he says. "It was an easy transition. I try to keep an open mind about everything. I was able to assimilate, learn the ropes quickly. The guys were very accommodating for a couple of weeks, and patient, but I got the hang of it. I had to learn the Spanish language. I had zero exposure to Chicano music growing up. I had to learn it on the fly, but I had good teachers. It didn't take long."

Steve Berlin recalls Los Super Seven's album being "a shot in the dark from the first day. I didn't know Max, Joel, or Ruben Ramos, but everybody got along really well. The music was fantastic, pretty joyous." Flaco adds, "It was just a bunch of guys getting together and playing some music, jamming . . . playing what we wanted."

Rick Trevino has such a great voice. You can listen to it for hours. It's a soothing, perfect pitch. I've toured with his band and he's toured with Los Texmaniacs. We just played at the Heinz Auditorium, in Houston, and Rick came to sing with us. He's a true professional, a great songwriter. He co-wrote "I Am a Mexican." When we recorded it for *Cruzando Borders*, I invited him to sing it. It fit right in. "I had been playing it with my band for a while,"

Max Baca and Josh Baca

Rick says. "When I wrote it, I was doing a show with Los Super Seven and Los Texmaniacs. It was the Super Bowl in Arizona. We played festivities the night before. When the gig was over, Flaco, Max, Josh, and I went to the hotel. We were having a few beers. I said, 'I want you guys to hear this song I just wrote—"I'm a Mexican."' I started playing it, more like a ranchera, an up-tempo thing. Flaco pulled out his accordion. Max pulled out his bajo sexto. I had my guitar. We were jamming. Flaco stopped the song and said, 'Hey Rick, let's slow it down.' At that point, I shut up and let Flaco do his thing. If he has something to say, I want to hear it. Max started playing those bolero riffs. The preproduction was done in a hotel room after the Super Seven show. I cut it with Flaco in Austin. When Max and the Texmaniacs tracked it, they came to Austin. The session was great. Max's take of the song was even more stripped-down than mine. He just had bajo sexto and accordion, which I loved. It sounded awesome."

Rick's father was a musician in Houston. Rick says, "There were three Texas big bands with brass sections mixing conjunto and pop music in the 1960s. My dad's band was Neto Perez & the Originals. The others were Ruben Ramos & the Revolution and Little Joe y Su Familia. They played everything from Blood, Sweat & Tears tunes to rancheras. I heard all of that when I was growing up, along with all the other pop music and country music."

Rick signed a five-album deal with Columbia Nashville in 1993. "I was playing a club, the Thirsty Turtle, in Largo Vista, Texas," he explains. "I had just finished my sophomore year in college. I was playing in restaurants and just starting to write songs. I was playing that tiny bar two or three times a month. The owners were super sweet. There was a big flood in 1992 and Lake Travis overflowed. A record executive from the pop division of Sony was vacationing in Largo Vista. There was no place for him to get something to eat but the Thirsty Turtle. He walked into the bar and got into a conversation with the owners. He asked if they had live music. The owners said, 'You've got to see this guy Rick Trevino.' They had advertising pictures of me on the wall. He said, 'I'll call Rick.' Sure enough, he went back to Boston and called me. He hadn't even heard my music. He said, 'I heard you're good. Can you send me some music?' I was in the middle of putting together a demo. I told him I wasn't done with it yet. When I finished it, he listened to the cassette tape of it and sent it, along with an eight-by-ten glossy headshot of me, to the head of CBS's A&R [artists and repertoire division], Steve Buckingham. It happened really fast. I got a call from Steve a few months later. He came to South by Southwest to hear some acts. He wanted to hear me; he liked my demo tape. He came to another Mexican cantina where I played. He listened to two songs and left. He left a message with my mom and dad, who were in the audience, saying, 'Meet me at the Four Seasons. Let's talk about getting a record deal going.'"

Rick's debut single, "Just Enough Rope (Bastante Cordón)" was the first mainstream country music single to be released in both English and Spanish. "She Can't Say I Didn't Cry" became a top-three country music hit. Rick's fourth album, *Learning as You Go*, in 1996, included two massive hits—the title track, which reached number two, and "Running Out of Reasons to Run," which topped the country music charts. "We did all three albums in English and Spanish," he says. "Since I'm third-generation Mexican American, my parents spoke fluent English. My grandparents spoke English. We're Texans. I was never forced to speak Spanish in the house. I'm still not good in conversation, but I can speak it. I can pronounce when I sing. I have the tongue."

He continues, "It was a business decision. I was concerned at the time. I didn't want people to think I was a Tejano singer or a Mexican artist crossing over to country music. I was hesitant about releasing another record in Spanish. I didn't want there to be any confusion as to who I was as an artist. As a kid, you stay away from your parents' music. Growing up, I kept an arm's length from Tejano music. I wanted to listen to rock & roll and country music. The label, though, was adamant that I record Spanish versions of my albums for Sony Discos. I was able to do it, so I did it. The problem was, they had different release schedules. They released the Spanish albums first."

He says of the Los Super Seven albums that they "came into my life at the right time. I was married with my first child. I wanted to get in touch with my Mexican roots. Los Super Seven was a great vehicle for that. I was happy to be included."

I was backstage one time with the Texas Tornados. Augie brought us all together and said, "When Freddy walks in, I'm going to tell him a joke. When I get to the punchline, everybody laugh."

Freddy walked in and Augie said, "Hey, Freddy, do you want to hear a joke?" "Okay, Augie, what is it?"

"Well, this guy goes into a café and asks the waitress what kind of pies they had. She says, 'We have apple pie, cherry pie, and pecan pie.' 'OK . . . give me a piece of that apple pie.'"

Augie started laughing. That was our cue. Everybody started laughing. Freddy started laughing. A few seconds later, he goes, "I didn't get it."

Augie retold the joke and we started laughing again. Freddy laughed along with us. Suddenly, he stopped. "Hey, wait a minute . . . I still don't get it!"

I told that story to Rick Trevino. He got a kick out it. Whenever he'd get a new guitarist, he'd say, "Max, let's get this guy. When he walks on the bus, tell that joke."

So, I did. When I got to the end of the joke, everybody started laughing and the new guitarist laughed too. I asked if he got it, and he said, "Yeah."

That made Rick laugh more. Since then, every time someone new comes around, Rick says, "Tell him the apple pie joke."

When Joel and I showed up at the studio, Freddy and David Hidalgo were already there. Steve Berlin's flight was delayed. He was supposed to get to the studio at eleven in the morning, but it turned out that he wouldn't get to Austin until four o'clock. While we waited, we decided to practice the songs. Dave McNair, the engineer, set up the mics. We started practicing these songs and Dave started recording. Freddy sang a song. Then Rick Trevino sang a song and Joe Ely did a song. Freddy did another song. When Steve Berlin finally got there, he played back what we had done and said, "That's not a rehearsal, that's a take." We had the basic tracks done.

Los Super Seven's album was a great weeklong project. Steve Berlin knew how to get the character out of each individual. He didn't say "play this" or "play that." He let everyone be themselves. That's how a great producer works. You capture the character of a person on tape; it doesn't become mechanical. When we were recording, we'd listen back to a track and they'd say, "What do you think, Max? We value your opinion." "I think it could use a little more harp on this song."

I came up with the Los Super Seven name. After we were done recording, I got called to the control room. "What would you call this band?" "It's simple. There are seven principal guys—the Super Seven." Their eyes opened and they went, "There it is!"

The first Super Seven album came out around the same time as Flaco's *Said and Done*. They both received Grammy Awards—*Said and Done* in the Tejano category and *Los Super Seven* in the Mexican/Mexican-American category. Everybody wanted to record with Flaco. He's magical. There's no other word to describe it. He takes his accordion out and he knows where to put the right notes and make it sound beautiful.

For the second Los Super Seven album, *Canto*, in 2001, Raul Malo (the Mavericks), Susana Baca, and Caetano Veloso replaced Flaco, Freddy, Joe Ely, Joel, and me. We returned for the third album, *Heard It on the X*, in 2005, but I was involved with the Texas Tornados and didn't go on the tour.

The Texas Tornados toured for a year and a half after Doug passed, but it wasn't the same. "We brought Doug's son, Shawn, into the band," says Augie, "but he said, 'I don't like to play that Mexican shit.' I told him, 'Just take your dad's place for a while. We'll find a guitar player.' He said, 'Okay.' He knew our songs. We did an album, ¡Está Bueno!, that released in 2010. Shawn stayed and took over the band. In 2017, we were booked to play in Colorado, Arizona, and California. The dates passed, so I called Shawn to see what was going on. He told me he had taken another band. I asked him why and he told me that Flaco and me were 'too old to play.'"

Flaco and I called the rest of the band and got them to quit, but we stayed in touch with Augie. Augie says: "A few months later, Flaco and I were booked to play in Sacramento as 'Formerly with the Texas Tornados.' Shawn called the promoter and said, 'I own the name. I copyrighted it.' He called Flaco and me and threatened to sue. I asked him why he had done that and told him that his father was probably rolling in his grave. He said, 'I'm going to do what I want to do.' Shawn was like a son to me; I was there when he was born. I haven't spoken to him since 2017 and I'll never talk to him again."

"Doug had an ego," says Flaco, "but he could talk to people. He was a professional in whatever he did. Shawn tried to copy him, but he didn't come close. Doug and I got together well. There were never contradictions, nothing heavy verbally, no fights. I always say that respect is the first thing. You have to have respect and get along with everybody."

When I moved to Austin, Óscar Téllez was living in Cotulla, about two and a half hours away. Further into the country from there, there's a lot of wildlife—pigs, deer, snakes—and a lot of brush. You're driving in the middle of nowhere, and suddenly boom! You come to the little town of Los Angeles, Texas, population ten. There's this bar, Ruby's Lounge, where conjuntos played during the weekend. Óscar worked at this bar—bartending and sweeping up.

One time, we played at a club in Austin. Flaco picked Óscar up and drove him to the gig. I told Óscar, "Man, I haven't seen you in a long time. Where've you been?"

Óscar told me that he'd been at Ruby's Lounge. "I know that place, we've played there. What are you doing?' 'I'm just helping out. The owner lets me sleep there." I asked him where he slept, and he told me on the pool table. What the hell? This was my idol, the greatest bajo sexto player in the world. What was he doing sleeping on a pool table? I felt so bad. I couldn't stand for that. I asked him to stay with me in my one-bedroom apartment. I offered him the sofa. He said, "Really, compadre?" That's what he always called me. I told him, "Of course." "That's awesome. Thank you, man"

Óscar didn't have a bajo sexto or a suitcase, just the clothes he was wearing, and they were rags. His boots were worn out. He had a pair of black pants that were faded. I took him to Walmart and bought him a couple pairs of pants, some shirts, t-shirts, underwear, and socks. He was really appreciative.

When we got home, he had to rest. He ended up getting the flu. While I was out doing gigs, he stayed on the sofa, under blankets, sweating it out. I gave him water and some food, but he didn't want to eat. He slept it off. Four or five days later, he finally got up. He had beaten it. I took him to get some chicken soup and he started getting his strength back.

The local musicians' union called, looking for Óscar. They had royalty checks for him but no idea where he was. I took him to the musicians' union the next day. He signed some papers and that was it. They gave him the $12,000 they had accumulated. He couldn't believe it. He was so happy. I told him to open a bank account and save the money, but he never knew that kind of life. When he was married, he had a beautiful home. He had cars, a bajo sexto, everything, but after he lost his wife, it all shifted. He gave up.

We had a gig with Flaco at Tipitina's and flew into New Orleans. We were taken to a hotel in a rough area and checked into our rooms. Óscar's room was next to mine. I turned the AC on. I needed to cool off. It was the middle of the summer and it was hot and humid. I heard a knock on my door. I opened it and a sweaty lady was standing there. "Sir, do you have a cigarette?" "No, ma'am, I don't smoke." "How 'bout a blowjob for five bucks?" "No, thank you, that's fine."

I shut my door and kicked back. Not even five minutes later, there was another knock on my door. I thought, "Oh my God, this lady doesn't understand what 'no' means."

I got up and opened the door, but it wasn't the lady. It was Óscar. He was standing there in his pants, barefoot, no shirt. He used to stutter. He looked at me and muttered, "C...C...compadre, you got five bucks you can lend me?"

Óscar had been in an auto accident. For the longest time, he didn't have teeth in the front. Finally, he met a woman who worked as a nurse and he started living with her. She bought him a set of partial dentures. They had hooks that clipped onto his remaining teeth. He looked sharp.

During the week, Óscar and I played local gigs for tips. In an hour, we could make ten or fifteen dollars apiece. Then we'd go to another place and do the same thing. That's how it is in Austin; there are so many musicians.

One night, a guy saw Óscar on stage and came up to me. He asked, "Who's that?" "His name's Óscar Téllez." "Well, I'm Robert Rodríguez. I'm producing a movie with Quentin Tarantino [*From Dusk to Dawn*] and I'd like him to be one of the main actors. Here's my card. Bring him to the auditions tomorrow morning."

I knew Óscar would be stoked. After we finished playing and got off the stage, I told him, "You're not going to believe this."

The next morning, I drove Óscar to where I had been told to take him. Sure enough, there was a long line of people. We went to the front and handed someone the card Robert Rodríguez had given me. We were the first ones in.

Óscar was photogenic; he had that "look." He went to the audition and came out with a script. He didn't blink an eye; he got the part. "I'm going to be in a movie!"

He was going to play a tough biker. The script was an inch thick and he had a lot to learn. I told him to practice his lines. He had a week to memorize his part. He tried, but he had only gone through the third grade. He could read, but memorizing all those lines was too tough for him.

The day before I was supposed to take him to do the movie, he called some of his friends and asked them to pick him up. I was busy doing a gig. When I got back to the apartment, he wasn't around. I thought he must have gone to the store. He called later that night and told me he was back at the bar. I guess he got cold feet.

He stayed in my apartment for a couple of weeks. Shortly after he moved out, my dad passed away. Óscar saw me at a gig with Flaco. He felt so bad about my dad. I had to go back to New Mexico for the funeral. He asked me for one of the prayer cards for my dad. He had known my dad really well.

When I got back from the funeral, I went to play with Flaco at the Tejano Conjunto Festival. Óscar was there with Mingo. I gave him the prayer card. He hugged me and started crying. I started crying. We got on stage with our eyes teary and red.

A week later, Mingo was scheduled to record. He had to pick Óscar up and take him to the studio. The night before, Óscar had been driving from the bar to the house where he was staying with the lady he had met. He had to go on this little country road. The truck he was driving must have hit a bump or something, and flipped over. He got ejected. This was about two or three a.m. They didn't find him until nine that morning. By then, the wild pigs had gotten him—the vultures, the coyotes. Parts of his body were scattered all over. It was a horrible death. His son had to identify him by body parts. They found his shirt. In the pocket was my dad's prayer.

Óscar was a funny guy, but when he got on stage, he got serious. He was an entertainer, a natural. It didn't matter what he played—bajo sexto or accordion. He was magical. He could make a trombone sound with his mouth and harmonize with his bajo sexto. It was amazing. I used to ask about licks that he played, but he could never remember what he had done. It came out naturally.

Freddy Fender struggled with diabetes and hepatitis C for years. He had a kidney transplant in 2002, with his daughter donating a kidney, and a liver transplant two years later. He performed his last concert on New Year's Eve 2005. He was going to have surgery to remove the upper left lobe of his lung because of a fungal infection, but surgeons found two large tumors and they left the lobe intact. A scan found nine more tumors. He started chemotherapy, but the side effects were too much and he stopped. In July, doctors detected two more tumors. Freddy told the Corpus Christi *Caller Times*, "I feel comfortable in my life. I'm one year away from seventy and I've had a good run."[1]

Freddy died at home on October 14, 2006. Two years before, he had told the Associated Press that the one thing that would make his musical career complete would be induction into the Country Music Hall of Fame in Nashville. "Hopefully, I'll be the first Mexican-American going into Hillbilly Heaven," he said.[2]

He would certainly qualify for the honor, but he and Johnny Rodríguez weren't the only Mexican Americans to make it in mainstream country music. Linda Ronstadt had massive hits. She came out of the pop scene, but she wanted to do something for her culture. She wanted to record the folk songs her dad had sung to her when she sat on his knee. The record company [Elektra/Asylum] said, "Are you out of your mind?," but she was persistent, and she made it happen. *Canciónes de Mi Padre* (Songs of My Father) sold millions of copies in late 1987. Linda Ronstadt used three of the best mariachi bands in the world—Mariachi Vargas de Tecalitlán, Mariachi los Camperos, and Mariachi los Galleros de Pedro Rey. It made a big impact.

It's the best-selling non–English language album of all time. It's still selling today. I was in my twenties when it came out. There's nothing that tops it. It was such a great production. Linda Ronstadt's voice was magical.

The first Mexican-American musician to break into the pop music mainstream, Ritchie Valens, scored several hit singles, including "Donna," "Come On Let's Go," and the traditional Mexican song "La Bamba" (from the state of Veracruz) before the February 1959 airplane crash that also took the lives of Buddy Holly and J. P. "The Big Bopper" Richardson. The same year, Montana-born Chan Romero, the son of a Spanish and Apache father and Mexican, Cherokee, and Irish mother, recorded the original version of "Hippy Hippy Shake." In 1960, San Francisco–born Eddie Quinteros recorded "Come Dance with Me."

Chris Montez, from Los Angeles, scored a top four hit in 1962 with "Let's Dance." A year later, Dallas-born Trini López scored with a Tejano version of "If I Had a Hammer." Sunny & the Sunglows, featuring San Antonio's Sunny Ozuna, had a mainstream pop hit with "Talk to Me." They appeared on *American Bandstand*, but Sunny returned almost exclusively to conjunto music.

Domingo "Sam the Sham" Samudio and his Dallas-based Sam the Sham & the Pharoahs matched their top-two 1965 hit "Wooly Bully" with "Li'l Red Riding Hood" a year later. Rudy Martínez of Michigan's ? & the Mysterians topped the charts with the organ-driven "96 Tears."

It was hard for Mexican American musicians because of discrimination. If your name was Peréz or Rodríguez, you couldn't get into the mainstream. Ritchie Valenzuela had to change his name to Ritchie Valens. A lot of Chicano artists did the same thing, but Carlos Santana was Santana. He stuck out with his guitar playing, but he played Latin rhythms. He broke into the mainstream. It's cool knowing that there was a Chicano musician at Woodstock. It opened the door for other Chicano artists—Freddy Fender, Johnny Rodríguez, and Los Lobos.

"When Los Lobos showed up on the scene," remembers Steve Berlin, "no Chicano band had been together for more than eighteen months or two years. Here come these guys who had been playing together for seven or eight years by that point. It was obvious that they had something unique and special. They played blues, rock, Cajun, zydeco, R&B, cumbias, boleros, and Norteños. That was the fun part. They liked to mix and match, a little of this, a little of that. That's always been our attitude. We're not one thing."

Los Lobos' first major-label album, *How Will the Wolf Survive?*, came out in 1984. They appeared on a track, "All Around the World, or the Myth of Fingerprints," on Paul Simon's *Graceland* album two years later. Their big break came the next year when they took a Mexican folk song, "La Bamba," and turned it into a million-selling rock tune. Ritchie Valens did it first, but his career hadn't lasted long. Steve Berlin says, "It was significant. Seemingly overnight, we were on everybody's lips. It's still our most-requested song."

TWELVE

SELENA

At the Tejano Music Awards after-party at the Hard Rock Café in San Antonio, the "Queen of Tejano Music," Selena (Quintanilla) (1971–1995) sang with the Texas Tornados. This native of Lake Jackson, Texas had scored nine consecutive "female vocalist of the year" awards. Cheap Trick headlined that night. The Texas Tornados opened up. For the grand finale, Cheap Trick invited Flaco, Freddy, and me back to the stage. Freddy sang "Wasted Days and Wasted Nights." Selena was in the crowd. Freddy looked at her and said, "I've known this woman since she was a little girl. She's got an amazing voice and a wonderful career ahead of her. Her name is Selena." People went crazy. She got up and asked, "What should we play?" She ended up singing the blues tune "C. C. Rider."

I knew Selena when she was getting started in the '80s. She came to Albuquerque. Los Hermanos Baca opened for her at local clubs. Her father, Abraham Quintanilla, did the sound. He was her manager. We loved opening for her, but our drummer didn't like it. Selena used electronic drums.

Los Hermanos Baca would get the crowd going and then Selena would do a big show. The last time we opened for her (1994), she had just signed a major endorsement deal with Coca-Cola. It was a big step for her. She had better equipment. Where she and her band had traveled in a van, now they had a bus.

We did a lot of shows with her. The Texas Tornados would headline. Back in those days, there was a Tejano musician, Roberto Pulido, who was hugely popular. He had saxophones, guitars, keyboards, and accordions in his band. Flaco and I did a show with him near Houston in 1994. Before we played,

Selena did a set, but the opening act was a singer from Santa Rosa, Texas, Ruben Vela, who would come out with a hit song, "El Coco Rayado," a year later. Radio played the shit out of it. For a conjunto cat in those days, getting exposure was tough. Conjunto musicians didn't get any recognition. There were no major labels to support them.

Selena wasn't at her peak yet. People loved her, and she had a big fan base, but she didn't get really popular until after her death. It was such a shame. She was working on her first English-language album (*Dreaming of You*) when she was killed, on March 31, 1995, by Yolanda Saldivar, a past president of her fan club and manager of her clothing line. *Dreaming of You* debuted at number one. The minute it was released, it shot to the top. Selena joined Janet Jackson and Mariah Carey as the only female artists to sell three hundred thousand copies of an album in its first week of release.

When I found out Selena had passed, I had just gotten home from being on the road with Flaco. We had just recorded with the Rolling Stones. I turned the news on, and they announced that Selena had been killed. I was floored. She was on her way to being huge.

The first female Tejano musician, Lydia Mendoza (1916–2007), recorded between 1928 and the 1980s. Kingsville, Texas–born Laura Canales (1954–2005) scored hits with Los Unicos, El Conjunto Bernal, Snowball & Company, Felicidad, and her own group, Laura Carnales & Encanto.

Then there was Selena. She cut her first records for local Tejano labels before signing with EMI Latin in 1981, Her self-titled debut was followed by *Ven Conmigo*, the first Tejano album by a female artist to achieve gold status. Her third solo album, *Entre a Mi Mundo*, sold more than three hundred thousand copies in 1992. *Amor Prohibido*, two years later, was the breakthrough, and Selena became only the second Tejano artist (after La Mafia) to sell half a million copies of an album.

Selena's magic was her genuineness, her humility. She was a sweetheart. Like most guys, I had a crush, but her dad was around all the time. We couldn't really talk. When we did, her dad would come over and break it up. But we remained friends. Whenever she'd see me, she'd give me a hug and a kiss on the cheek. She was down to earth. Nothing went to her head, like some Tejano artists who have a song on the radio and become their biggest fan.

When she was young, she didn't speak Spanish. Her father made the decision for her to sing in Spanish. When he was younger, he had a hard time.

Conjunto music was thought of as cantina music or campfire music. It never got respect. Selena's father tried playing clubs, but people were resistant. He didn't want his daughter to go through that. He thought if she sang in Spanish, she could play for her people.

Selena learned lyrics phonetically, but she put passion in everything she did. That overcame anything else, whether she spoke Spanish or not. She got the message of her songs across, all heart and soul. Eventually she learned Spanish and knew what she was singing. It made a difference. She went to Mexico and performed in Monterrey and Nueva León. The music speaks for itself.

After Selena's death, her brother, A. B. Quintanilla, joined Corpus Christi–born keyboards player Cruz Martínez in the electronic cumbia-meets-hip-hop group the Kumbia Kings. After they split, Quintanilla formed the Kumbia All-Starz, while Martínez assembled the equally dynamic Los Super Reyes.

The modern side of Tejano music isn't my cup of tea, groups like Mazz and La Mafia, with synthesizers, lights, and people dancing on the stage. To me, that takes away the heart of the music. It's just sugar-coating, like putting a Band-Aid on a gunshot wound. When you talk about conjunto music, that's the real deal. It's home-grown and authentic.

THIRTEEN

LOS TEXMANIACS

I formed Los Texmaniacs in 1997, with the concept of playing traditional conjunto roots music but going out of the box with a little rock & roll and blues. It's upbeat, happy sounding music—música allegre. When you hear a polka, it's not sad. It's "Let's drink a beer and have fun" music.

Los Texmaniacs did it the hard way, going from town to town, country to country, trying to earn respect through our music, not because we had a flashy theatrical show. We don't wear tight jeans or shake our asses. Of course, it's important to be in shape—to look as good as we can—but I'm no Elvis Presley. I'm overweight, but when I get on stage, it's about making beautiful music, not what I look like.

The only airplay we get comes from National Public Radio and a few Americana stations. There really aren't any more Tejano stations. If they play our music, it'll usually be the older stuff, not our latest CD. It's hard to build a fan base without a radio hit.

When I formed Los Texmaniacs, I had Israel "Speedy" Villanueva on bass and Joel Guzman on drums. Pete Ybarra played accordion for the first gigs, but he left to play with Tejano superstar Emilio Navarra. Michael Guerra took his place. Michael plays with the Mavericks now. We met in California when he was fifteen or sixteen. I was touring with the Texas Tornados. I saw him playing with his father and his sister. They had a family conjunto. I could see how talented he was. We became friends. The first time he called me, he couldn't believe he had my phone number. He was so excited. He asked, "If I move to San Antonio, can I play with you?" I told him he could do that after he finished school and made his parents proud. "Get an education, there's always time for music."

Michael ended up graduating. Two weeks later, he flew to Austin. He stayed with me for a while. I got him a gig playing part-time with Ruben Ramos & the Mexican Revolution. I played with Ruben from time to time. I also got him a gig playing with me in Rick Trevino's band. Michael would go off and play with other bands. We'd get back together as Los Texmaniacs.

After Doug Sahm's death in 1999, I wanted to relight the spark of the Texas Tornados. It wasn't the same without Doug. That's when I decided to make my own band. I was going to call it "the Texas Twisters," but there was already a band with that name. At the time, the band 10,000 Maniacs was popular. I wanted to keep the name Texas, so I put it together with 10,000 Maniacs and came up with Texas Maniacs . . . Texmaniacs.

We were a really good band. We rocked out at cantinas in Austin. We got noticed and started playing in San Antonio. We played semiregularly at Saluté International Bar, home of Esteban "Steve" Jordan, the great accordion wizard, until it closed in 2012.

My favorite place to play was Ruben's Place in Selma, Texas. Pedro Silva Castro and his wife, Maria, opened it in 1939 as a grocery store and gas station. Bands played on the patio. Their son, Ruben, took it over. It was a cool spot. We did a few photo shoots there; Flaco made a few videos. It was right off I-35 and musicians would stop by. It was a good watering hole. They had a jukebox with nothing but conjunto 45s—the old pioneers, some great music.

During the week, if I wanted to go out, drink a beer, and shoot some pool, I'd go to Ruben's Place. Of course, on the weekends, Los Texmaniacs played there. We played the November 2013 closing night with Flaco, Mingo Saldivar, and Mark Weber y Los Cuernos. Lorenzo Martínez says, "We were always learning, whether we were playing at a jam or a dance. Watching how people danced, how they grooved to our music, taught us. It was a cycle; they gave energy to the band."

After recording *Tex-Mex Groove* in 2004, we released it on my label, Maniax Records. Michael was on accordion. Speedy Villanueva played bass; he was a rocker. He brought so much firepower to the band. He was always pushing it. We had a drummer (Chente Barrera) who helped us from time to time, but he had his own group going on. We had a lot of energy for a four-piece band.

There were some great guests on the album. Flaco and Ruben Ramos did songs. David Hidalgo and Cesar Rosas from Los Lobos came to do a song and ended up doing three. One was Sir Douglas Quintet's "She's About a Mover." David played guitar and Cesar sang. It was a really great version. It gave us a boost. I did a slide bajo sexto run in the beginning, like I was playing bottleneck.

David Hidalgo wanted a güiro for "She's About a Mover." He thought it'd sound good. We didn't have much time; they had to go to do a show that night. The studio didn't have a güiro. David asked if we had a Solo plastic cup and we managed to find one. It had little baby ridges, like the ridges on a güiro. Then David took a plastic fork and broke all the tines off but one. He said, "Crank up the microphone," and played a güiro solo with the cup and fork. It worked. It sounded like a güiro. That's part of Los Lobos' black magic, David doing things like that.

I've known Los Lobos since I was a kid, listening to them whenever they toured New Mexico. The Baca Brothers opened for them in Santa Fe, right after they came out with "La Bamba" in 1987. It was a huge concert at a baseball field. It was packed. The guy who was booking Peter Rowan when I was twelve years old booked Los Lobos. He had the Baca Brothers open for them. Through the years, we stayed in touch. When I toured with the Texas Tornados, we did shows together. Los Lobos has remained the same band for more than forty years—the same unit. You have to admire that. There're no egos in that band. Everyone is a superstar. Everyone contributes.

I worked with David Hidalgo, Cesar Rosas, and Steve Berlin on the Los Super Seven project, but they recorded on my album and didn't charge me a dime. I offered to pay them, but they were so humble. They said, "No, Max, you're going to insult us if you pay us to record with you. We dig you."

Lorenzo Martínez joined Los Texmaniacs shortly after our first album. He's a disciplined, heartfelt musician. He loves mariachi music and sings beautiful boleros. You don't hear that kind of music any more, with beautiful three-part harmonies and two or three guitars. When we met, he was playing drums. I didn't know he also played acoustic stringed instruments. He can also make beautiful music on a güiro. The only way to describe him is "puro corazón." He's pure heart, a genuine musician. He's like Flaco, true to who he is—Chicano. He shines. "Playing with Max and Los Texmaniacs started out as a lot of fun," Lorenzo remembers. "We were meeting a lot of people, creating great music, gaining confidence and knowledge, and becoming our own as musicians and a group."

Michael Guerra decided to do his own thing and left the band. Josh says, "It got to be about egos. Everybody was already a star with other groups."

I talked to a few accordion players, looking for one who would fit. I had always been a fan of David Farías. He's five years older than me—my brother's age. When we were teenagers, my brother and I searched for different conjuntos. We listened to the pioneers like Tony De la Rosa, Valerio Longoria, Mingo Saldivar, and, of course, Flaco. Then we came across Los Hermanos Farías. They had a similar name to ours, so I started listening to them and became a big fan of David. He's blessed with a great voice.

David worked as a custodian at the airport. I'd see him when I'd get off a plane. We'd walk to the baggage claim and talk. I thought he was such a cool, humble guy. We exchanged phone numbers. Then, all of sudden, this big Tejano explosion started happening. At the front of it was La Tropa F, the band that David was playing with. They had changed their name from Los Hermanos Farías, but still included David's father, Joe, on bajo sexto, and his brothers. La Tropa F recorded for a major label, EMI Latin/Capitol, and had number one hits on Tejano radio. Their album *Right on Track* received a Tejano Music Award as the best album of 1993. "We were more progressive,"

Max Baca and David Farías

Los Texmaniacs

David explains, "with keyboards and synthesizers. My brother, Juan, started writing songs. We started recording different kinds of cumbias and rancheras. When we recorded for Manny Records before switching to EMI Latin/Capitol, they had us change our name to La Tropa F. Remember that TV show, *F Troop*? A couple of DJs gave us the name. I didn't think it was a good idea. We were Los Hermanos Farías for a long time. 'No, no, no, it's gonna work.' It really took off. We played a lot of family parties. They were a lot of fun."

David's father and uncle (Jesse Hernandez) were Los Compadres Farías. In David's words, "On the bass was my older brother, Joe, and, my next older brother, Johnny, played drums. Joe taught all of us. He said, 'You're going to get the accordion, you're going to get the keyboard,' and so on. He taught me to sing."

La Tropa F had a huge hit, "Juan Sabor," in 1995. "It put us on the map," David recalls. "There were lines to get into our concerts. It was crowded every night and we were playing five or six nights a week. We had two buses and an eighteen-wheeler, a lot of people working for us. It went on for fifteen years."

I went to the Tejano Music Awards ceremony. I had been nominated as the year's best bajo sexto player. I ran into David and he said, "Hey man, how's it going?" "My accordion player has just left the band and I'm looking for someone to replace him." He said, "That's funny. My brothers just fired me."

"Problems between brothers were going on," David explains, "about money and all the things that came with it." They ended up firing him. "They sent me a letter and told me that I had so many days to answer. I talked to my mom and dad about it, but I didn't respond to the letter. A week later, we had the awards show. That's where I met Max. He was a little down. 'What's wrong?,' I asked him. He told me that his accordion player was quitting. 'What timing, I just got fired!' Soon after that night, Los Texmaniacs toured in Europe. He asked me to come."

David played with us for seven years and contributed a lot. He's a real showman with amazing stage presence. Whatever gig he plays, whether it's a party, a little club on the West Side, or a show for ten thousand people, he gives 100 percent. He loves music, an old-school musician from the school of hard knocks. He wasn't doing it just for the money.

Soon after he came into the band, he told me, "I'm learning more and more about my accordion." He had to step it up. With his brothers, he played the same thing every night. With Los Texmaniacs, he had to play differently every show, with longer riffs and more jazzy things. He remembers that at

Los Texmaniacs

his first Los Texmaniacs gig, "Max said, 'We're going to do 'Low Rider.' 'The song by War?' 'Yeah.' I never played the songs I did with Max before. I had my style, music I played, it was a totally different deal. I have a lot of faith when I do projects. I said to myself, 'This is going to work,' and it did. It took time for us to mesh together but it worked."

We had real firepower with David on accordion, Speedy on bass, and Lorenzo on drums. David had a different style than Michael, but he was able to adapt to Los Texmaniacs' music. "The coolest thing," he says, "was that we didn't rehearse."

For a while, we had a guitar player, William James "Willie J" Laws. He used to play every Sunday in a juke joint in San Antonio. I'd see him every chance I got. He called me one time and asked me to sit in with him. He told me to bring my bajo sexto. It was hardcore blues music. This guy was the real deal. I called him "The Bluesman." Sitting in with him was like going to school. He had opened shows for B. B. King, Etta James, Buddy Guy, and Willie Nelson. I learned a lot from him. He was such a nice guy. He loved to play with Los Texmaniacs and became our guitar player for a while. He played on *Live in Texas*. On the recording, we featured him on a song. In the middle, we broke it down. He did a lick and I answered with a lick. After he moved to Boston, he stopped playing with us as much, but he came with us to Europe.

We hit a dry spell and didn't record for two or three years. Finally we said, "Man, it's about time." That's why we titled the CD *About Time*. We didn't mean anything more than that. We laughed about it. It was more of a traditional conjunto album and we got a couple of songs on Tejano radio. Tejano music's popularity was booming.

Speedy quit after *About Time* came out and I got another bass player, Óscar García. I knew him for years. He's actually an accordion player, a bajo sexto player, a drummer, and a bass player, a good conjunto musician.

Changing musicians is tough. You create a sound with a certain unit and then you have to get a replacement and start all over. Through the years, Los Texmaniacs has gone through different accordion players, different drummers, different bass players.

I'd talk to Flaco and ask for his advice. He'd tell me, "Just be who you are." You have to keep what you believe in and who you are. No matter who's playing with me, it has to be a Texmaniacs sound. That speaks for itself. Uncle Carl told me, "You can replace the doors on a car, change an engine, but you're the heart and soul of Los Texmaniacs. You only have to play one note and it makes a difference. You don't have to be flashy, progressively skilled, or precise. That's just mechanical, but if you feel those notes, you can make your instrument respond."

Flaco picked up his accordion and said, "Close your eyes; make this song cry." He told me to make my instrument respond to how I'm feeling. It meant so much to me. It's how I've gotten through my life and my career—through my heart.

Los Texmaniacs recorded *Live in Texas* at the Tejano Conjunto Festival. There were six or seven thousand people in the crowd. Not long after putting Los Texmaniacs together, I had called Juan Tejeda and asked if we could play at the festival. Fortunately he had seen us playing at a local bar and loved us. He booked us for Sunday evening. We let the crowd know we were going to be recording. We asked them to cheer.

GRABACIÓN
(Recording)

My dream was to record on the Smithsonian Folkways label, but they don't choose just anybody. They record only the best of the best. They're the real deal. I wanted to be part of that, so I kept submitting three- or four-song demos to Daniel Sheehy, who was then director of Smithsonian Folkways. I started when I was still in Albuquerque playing with my brother. I would polish them up, but he'd say, "Max, you sound great, but you need a concept."

There has to be a concept to everything that you do. That way, it's going to mean something and have structure. Without a concept, you're just spinning your wheels. I thought about it before hiring David Farías to play. I thought he'd fit in because I was already a fan of his. We have a lot in common. We play the same music in the same style. We never rehearsed. It was "C'mon, let's just play the gig. We've done this all our lives—let's have fun and make music." It jelled.

Daniel Sheehy explains, "The Smithsonian has a special fund, the Latino Initiatives Pool, to encourage programming for Latin-Americans. After I came aboard, I applied for a grant each year. I got one a year for eighteen years. My boss knew I liked doing projects with Latino music. The concept behind Smithsonian Folkways' Traditionales series was to record music that was more than music, music that represented people, music that had an identity. When Max first approached me, it wasn't that the time wasn't right, it was a matter of whether I had grant funding to subsidize the project. When we got the money, we were ready to go."

It took thirty years before Daniel Sheehy said, "Now you have a concept" and signed Los Texmaniacs to Smithsonian Folkways. We were ready. Our first Smithsonian Folkways album, *Borders y Bailes*, won the "Best Tejano

Album of 2009" Grammy. We recorded songs from the borderland, not necessarily about crossing the border, but songs we played at dances, songs we'd been playing all our lives. We didn't have to rehearse them. We just added Texmaniacs power to them. This is who we are and what we do. We recorded live in the studio, in the old style, without overdubs. We captured the moment. What you hear is what you get.

The album had the right material. We played polkas, schottisches, redovas, cumbias, and boleros. Pete Reiniger, the studio engineer who recorded and mixed the album, made it flow. He started it with the hard-driving "Marina" to catch listeners' attention and keep them from getting bored. You didn't hear polka, polka, polka, and then, all of a sudden, a bolero. He made it flow so when you listened to the whole album, it would be pleasing. When it finishes, you want to hear it again.

"Marina" is an Italian song written and recorded in 1959 by Italian-Belgian accordion player Rocco Granata. Flaco recorded it on *Partners*. I've always loved the song. It's simple, but it's got so much meaning. "Marina, Marina, Marina, I love you with all of my heart. My love for you, dear, is forever." That's the whole song. We played it at the fortieth anniversary celebration of *A Prairie Home Companion*. Garrison Keillor invited us to Minnesota to be part of that special show. I remember driving back to the hotel and getting a phone call from a number I didn't recognize. I answered the phone. "Hello, is this Mr. Baca?"

The lady on the other end of the phone was in tears. She said, "Oh, my God, I want to thank you so much for playing my song."

I asked, "What do you mean?" and she continued to tell me, "I'm eighty-seven years old. My grandfather wrote that song to me. My name's Marina."

She hadn't heard it since her grandfather wrote it.

"A Mover el Bote" is a more recent cumbia. It's slang—"Shake Your Booty." It's like the limbo: everybody can catch on to it. Mario Quintero Lara recorded it with Los Tuscanes de Tijuana (the Tuscans of Tijuana) and the Texas Tornados included it on *Live from the Limo*.

"Canción Mixteca" was a Mexican Revolution song. José López Álvarez wrote its melody in 1912 and added the lyrics about being homesick for his Oaxacan home after moving to Mexico City three years later. Ry Cooder played it on the soundtrack of Wim Wenders' *Paris, Texas* (1984) with Harry Dean Stanton singing it. Lila Downs recorded it in 1999.

We didn't overthink the recording. We just went into the studio, put our instruments on, and started playing. We had a list of songs and we played them heartfelt and sincere. That's how the album came out. There was a story behind every song.

Daniel Sheehy was a second dad to us. He took a liking to me and the band. We stayed at his house. His wife hired us one year to surprise him for his birthday. I told her we didn't need to get paid. We wanted to do it because we loved him. She flew us to Washington, DC. Their son picked us up and brought us to their house. Daniel was busy barbecuing. We went over to him and starting singing. He was so happy. He's truly something else, a real treasure. I owe a lot to him.

Borders y Bailes was a folkloric album, but I played bajo sexto riffs that were bluesy and jazzy. I put my own twist to it. The accordion player added flashy licks. It had Texmaniacs out-of-the-box spirit, but in a traditional way. In the liner notes, Daniel Sheehy wrote, "Los Texmaniacs breathe new air into conjunto music."

We had a refreshing sound. Daniel Sheehy once asked me to describe Los Texmaniacs' music and I told him, "It's hip music that everyone can relate to."

"We had cameras rolling through the recording session," Daniel Sheehy remembers, with Charlie Weber as the cameraman. "We had four days to record the basic tracks. Later, there was mixing, mastering, and touch-ups that were needed. We were limited by time, but we didn't cut corners. If something wasn't right, we worked on it and made sure that it was. It was a lot of fun. Max is a personality; everybody knows that. He might show up two hours later than he was supposed to, but everyone who knows him just shakes their head and laughs—that's Max. But he's very much in control as an artist. He follows his inner voice. That's one of the things that makes him special as a creator. He brings people together from diverse cultures. He and Josh are from Albuquerque, but they've aspired to be Tejano musicians. Noel Hernandez is from the Rio Grande Valley, engrained in tradition. Lorenzo Martínez grew up listening to traditional music, but also has that West Coast sensibility. When you have different people, with everyone bringing something else to the table, that's when you have a delicious feast."

We recorded at Blue Cat Studio. Pete Reiniger was the engineer. "I put my first studio together in a backyard in 1984," says Joe Treviño, "Two years later, I went to Elephant Tracks Studio, where I met Max, and stayed there until 1999. Since then, the studio is where it's now at 1311 South Presa Street."

Noel Hernandez

I was in the studio, adding bajo sexto to a project. It was about midnight. My phone kept ringing off the hook. I had it on silence, but I could feel the vibration. I looked at my phone to see who it was. It was a writer for the *San Antonio Express-News*. I told the engineer, "Let me take a break and see what's going on." When I called the writer, he said, "Congratulations, Max. You've been nominated for a Grammy."

I went home after we finished recording. My mom was visiting from Albuquerque. I was so happy. I told her about the nomination, and she started crying tears of joy. She gave me a big hug. She said, "Your dad would be so proud of you."

I went to the 52nd Grammy Award ceremonies on January 10, 2010 at the Staples Center in Los Angeles, with my sister, my son, and the guys in the band—David Farías, Lorenzo Martínez, and Óscar García. We dressed in black ties, tuxedos, and black hats. We sat fifteen rows from the stage and watched the show. Then it was time for the category we were in, "Best Tejano Album." They listed all the nominees and then said, "The winner is Los Texmaniacs."

My heart fell to the ground. Everyone had been telling me that I was going to win. They'd say, "You'd better have a speech prepared," but I'd think, "I'm not going to make a speech. If we win, we win."

"We got all dressed up," remembers Lorenzo, "but we said that what would happen would happen. We were so blessed and thankful to Dan Sheehy and Smithsonian Folkways. We had gotten to a lot of bridges that didn't happen, and almost jumped off, but they built the bridge that got us across."

When they called our name as the winner of the Grammy, my son Carlos jumped up and yelled. My sister made all kinds of noises. The whole audience was cheering. I just stood there, not knowing what to do. I remember my sister telling me, "Go to the stage."

I started walking to the stage. Every step brought flashbacks of when I was a kid playing with my dad and my brother, of being stranded in Santa Rita when the Red Cross had to come—all those memories. I finally made it to the stage and walked up the steps, the guys behind me.

David remembers of that same moment, "All I heard was my wife screaming. I was in shock. Then I saw Max three hundred feet in front of me, running. 'Hey, wait for me!'"

The band playing stopped. The presenters handed me the Grammy and said, "Congratulations." I stood by the podium, holding the Grammy. My heart was thumping. Grammys are the highest achievement for a musician. Getting a nomination as one of the top five is like winning the division championship. Winning the Grammy is like winning the Super Bowl.

There were thousands of people there—Lady Gaga, Beyoncé, and all these celebrities—but there was dead silence. The whole audience was looking at me. I didn't have a speech prepared. You know the first thing I said? "How about those Dallas Cowboys?" I didn't know what else to say. That was the first thing that came out of my mouth. Everybody started laughing. It broke the ice. I went on to say, "I want to thank God. I'm going to dedicate this to my father up in Heaven." I thanked Daniel Sheehy, Flaco, everybody I could think of. We only had so many minutes and I had to let my bandmates say something, too.

When we walked off the stage, people stood up and clapped. They felt the humbleness we had when we spoke.

We had to walk the red carpet. We followed it to a room backstage and were shown where to stand. There were over a hundred photographers flashing all over the place. Reporters asked me about conjunto music, and I explained it in a nutshell. We walked the red carpet again and went to another room where there was more press. It took an hour before we got back to the Grammy show.

Lorenzo remembers, "It was a great event, taking a lot of pictures, meeting musical stars. We met Smokey Robinson and Will Smith. We met musicians from Texas I had never met before. Little Joe y Su Familia were there. They play the orchestral style of conjunto. We shared time with him and Ruben Ramos from Austin."

I wish my dad could have been there, though he was in spirit. I felt his presence as I was walking to that stage.

We went to the reception after the awards ceremony. All these superstars were there. David and I stood there, talking to people. I was starstruck.

We shook hands with Carlos Santana. A group of women walked by and started screaming, "Oh, my God, oh my God!" They asked David and me if they could take our photo. I told them, "Sure." They started taking photos and a couple of their friends joined them. Now, there were five girls taking pictures of us and saying, "We love you guys, thank you so much." As they were walking away, we heard one of the girls ask another, "Who are those guys anyway?" "Oh, that was Brooks & Dunn."

For the longest time, I wouldn't hang up my awards. I kept them in a closet. I felt like I didn't deserve them, I guess. I was young and there were bajo sexto players older than me who had been playing for years and years.

Once Óscar Téllez was in the kitchen in my house. He asked me where my Rolling Stones double-platinum record was. He wanted to see it. I told him it was in the closet. He hit the table hard with his hands and said, "What are you doing?" I told him that he was my idol and that he should have these awards. He hit the table again and said, "You deserve these. You did it. I'm proud of you."

I started crying. Óscar never got anything until after he died. They put him in the Conjunto Hall of Fame, but he didn't get to enjoy that.

He told me that I was the one taking the bajo sexto to the next level and demanded that I hang up all my awards and certificates. We got everything out of the closet, and he helped me hang them up. When I walk into my house and look at my awards, I stop and think. They have meaning. Each one has a memory. They make me proud. They were a lot of hard work. They're an accomplishment.

Another traditional album, *Texas Towns and Tex-Mex Sounds*, followed *Borders y Bailes*. It got a "Best Latin Album" nomination. All of the songs were about Texas—Marty Robbins' "El Paso" and Bob Wills & the Texas Playboys' "San Antonio Rose." We were honored to get Ray Benson from Asleep at the Wheel to sing on it. We did a couple of songs by Flaco's father, Don Santiago Jiménez—"Ay Te Dejo en San Antonio" (I'm Gonna Leave You in San Antonio), which opened the album, and "Viva Seguín," the tune I heard Flaco playing on *Saturday Night Live*.

Soon after the album came out, David Farías came to me and said, "Compadre, I think it's time for me to go back to my brothers." I told him, "That's fine, good luck. We had a good run." (David explains, "I had been playing with Max and Los Texmaniacs and doing my own thing at the same time. I had two bands. I got so busy that I told Max I had to bow out. I thanked him for everything he had done for me, but I decided to go by myself.")

We still talk to each other. If Josh can't make a gig, David's the first guy I'll call. We went through a lot in seven years.

Josh comments, "I've always been a fan of David's. I loved La Tropa F. They were always on the radio, hit after hit. I didn't really know Los Hermanos Farías; they were an older group. Honestly, from the bottom of my heart, when I found out that David Farías was going to be the accordion player for Los Texmaniacs, I wasn't into it. I was a kid. Maybe I didn't know any better, but it didn't fit my vibe, the energy that Los Texmaniacs was asking for. He played differently. The sound changed."

When he replaced David, Josh's "mind was in a different dimension. I left Albuquerque and moved to San Antonio when I was seventeen years old," he recalled, "and started playing with a local musician. It was the same set every night, with click tracks and pyrotechnics. I had to play the same lick in the same spot every time, the same dance movement. If I was off by one step, it'd mess up the entire show. I stuck with that for five years, but my soul, my heart, and my love for music was Los Texmaniacs, Los Hermanos Baca, and Flaco Jiménez music—folk music. At the time, I was in need. I was about to have my daughter and my son was still at home. I needed to work and provide for my family. I don't have an education. I didn't graduate. My grandfather was an accountant and tax preparer, but I've played music since I was young. I played mariachi music in bars. I played accordion, keyboards, bajo sexto, bass, drums, whatever was needed. If I didn't know how to play them, I'd take a lesson and learn the basics. I had to make a living."

Josh played with us from the time he was a little kid. "I'd hang out with them at house parties," he recalls, "and we'd jam. I'd see Los Texmaniacs at a club and they'd call me up to play. The chemistry was there—family. My uncle told me, 'We're not rock & rolling it. We've got a lot of folk festivals. We need to play traditional music.' I knew the songs. I had to just go over them, practicing, practicing, practicing. In the beginning, I tried playing like David, that attitude. Finally, Flaco told me, 'You're not David.' He said I had to find myself—'Feel it and be who you are.' At first, I had timing issues if it wasn't click-tracked. I'd speed up or slow down. It took a month before I said, 'I've got it.' I learned songs my uncle had wanted to play but hadn't had an accordion player capable of playing them."

Josh started going to Flaco's house every day: "I'd be there for hours hanging out and watching him repair accordions. He showed me things on the accordion, saying, 'Do it like this—in, out, in, out—boom!' It's a different attitude."

For Los Texmaniacs' *Tex-Mex Groove*, my idea was a cross between the Texas Tornados and Los Lobos with more conjunto elements. There'll never be another Texas Tornados. There's only one Doug Sahm, one Augie Meyers, one Flaco Jiménez, and one Freddy Fender. I had to be myself. We included rock tunes on the album, which was very cool, but we didn't overdo it. It was more Americana-sounding. We recorded Bruce Channel's "Hey Baby!" It was a great album. People still ask for it.

When I met Noel Hernandez, in 1996, he had been playing bass for Elida Reyna's Elida y Avante for ten years. They did the conjunto circuit in Texas. Born in 1971, he had grown up in Weslaco, a South Texas farming community close to the border. "There's a lot of citrus there," he says. "My grandparents on my dad's side were born in that area. They were into farming. Of course, they were influenced by other farmers who were Czech, Polish, and German. There was a need for an accordion. My dad was interested in that sound. He was born in 1939. When he was a teenager, he dropped out of school. He preferred working. He had a fascination for farming equipment. My dad was the 'Tractor Whisperer,' you could say."

When the United States signed the Mexican Farm Labor Agreement with Mexico in 1942, they established the bracero (manual laborer) program. Noel recalls, "Mexican workers were brought in during harvest season. My grandpop was a foreman. In the evenings, my dad would hang out with him. There'd be guitars, violins, and clarinets. They had a big bass drum and they would march around the streets to notify people that there was going to be a jam session. My dad got an accordion when he was fourteen or fifteen. He learned from people from Mexico, but he also learned from other musicians like Narciso Martínez. When I was a kid, all of our neighbors had accordions instead of a piano. I used my dad's accordion for a stepladder to reach my cereal. It was always around the house. Every Friday and Saturday, my dad got together with family and friends to play music on our front porch. It was mostly instrumental—polkas, redovas, and schottisches. I listened to mariachi and Norteño music on the radio, but I also listened to Hank Williams, Willie Nelson, and the pop hits of the era—the Eagles, the Beatles. My older brother saw that I was interested in music. He played guitar. He taught me a bass line for a polka and a few different conjunto rhythms. I caught on right away. I was twelve years old. As soon as I learned how to accompany, I was onto it. My mom bought me a Harmony guitar. I used it as my bass. I joined my first band because I didn't have a bass. They did. It wasn't pure conjunto music, more of a hybrid. It involved a lot of keyboard and guitar. Dancing was a big factor. If people didn't get up to dance by the second song, we'd think about what would do it. People knew the steps to rhythms we played, but it didn't matter. If you don't know the steps, create your own. It's all welcomed."

In high school, Noel joined a guitar group: "Imagine a choir of guitars. We sang traditional Mexican songs. I played upright bass. I was hungry for all kinds of music, so I studied for a while at the university in Edinburg, Texas. I didn't want to be a teacher, but learn music theory. I met a singer, Elida Reyna, and we formed a Tejano band. We had an accordion player. It was based on conjunto music, but we added other flavors. I arranged the music. We toured through the 1990s, traveling through Texas and some of the US, performing at clubs and festivals."

I met saxophonist/producer Steve Berlin (Los Lobos) around 1999, in Houston. He recalls, "We had a truck with a lighting system and a PA, so we'd get to a venue early to set up. That night, the closing act was Flaco Jiménez and his Conjunto. Max was playing bass for them. He came up to me and introduced himself. They had just come from the Grammy ceremonies in Los Angeles. Flaco had won a Grammy. I was a big fan of Flaco's music. My dad had vinyl records of all of the pioneers."

Flaco and I had flown to Houston to do the show, but our instruments hadn't made the flight. Noel is so humble, he offered his bass to me. It was an awesome jazz bass. He still has it.

"Max stayed in touch afterwards," says Noel. "He never failed to call once in a while and say, 'Hey man, what's going on? Who are you playing with?' I'll never forget that. It's one sign of a true friend. I remember when he formed Los Texmaniacs in 1997. He called to see what I was up to. I was playing with Elida y Avante, but he offered me a gig as a bass player. I was honored. I knew Max played bajo sexto, but I hadn't heard him. He was playing bass when we met. I finally heard him and wow! He could really play. He had a beautiful sound. I heard the Óscar Téllez influence, which I really dug."

After leaving Elida y Avante, Noel formed his own six-piece band, Los Frijoles Románticos (the Romantic Beans). They were a good band, very versatile. They played rock, cumbia, Latin funk, and ballads. Noel was the director. Their self-named 2004 album was nominated for a "Best Tejano Album" Grammy.

Noel says, "I grew up listening to conjunto music. My dad had a big vinyl collection. He'd listen to them while drinking beer, hanging with the family and relatives. I was always around my dad. He'd buy me toy tractors. I'd be playing with them while he listened to Tony De la Rosa or Narciso Martínez. I'm blessed to have his collection. That was one influence, but we lived close to the border and I got to hear mariachi music and other kinds of wonderful sounds that came from Mexico. You could trace them back to the Caribbean and Africa. My mom bought me a transistor radio when I was seven years old. I remember listening to Hank Williams and Willie Nelson, the Eagles, the Beatles, jazz, the blues, and honky-tonk. There's no way I could play in a band that only played one genre. It'd feel like prison."

When Óscar García quit Los Texmaniacs, I needed somebody to replace him on bass. It wasn't easy. We needed a bassist who could play hardcore conjunto with feeling and then jump to a blues shuffle or a rock & roll song with heart and soul. There are few bass players who could do that. Noel was my first choice. I asked him if he'd be interested in doing some shows with us, so he came down and played with us. I took him to Switzerland for a tour.

"I wasn't touring at the time," Noel remembers, "but running a restaurant with my brother. It was a totally committed job. I told my brother that I wanted to play music . . . I had to do it. I went on the tour and the gigs felt great. I enjoyed the life."

About a year or so later, I asked Noel to play bass on Los Texmaniacs' East Coast tour. "We played at the 2013 Rhythm & Roots Festival in Rhode Island," he says, "and the Library of Congress in Washington, DC. We played at the Black Pot Cook-Off in Louisiana. I was blown away by the reaction that we got. Playing with bands in South Texas, we had always drawn a Hispanic crowd, which is beautiful, but playing with Max, we were playing for all kinds of people. That blew my mind. It was just what I wanted. It turned me on to be playing music I grew up with for people from all parts of the world."

After the tour, I asked Noel to join Los Texmaniacs. He says, "I really wanted to, but I had a business going. It took a lot of my time, but I eventually worked it out where I was able to work with Max and the band. I told him to send me the material so I could go over it. He said, 'No man, don't worry about it. You've got it covered.'"

En route to Noel's first gig, "Max turned to me and asked, 'Can you sing harmony?' 'Whoa!' I could sing harmony, but I can't remember lyrics. I told him, 'I don't know the songs you're singing,' but I crammed and learned them as well as I could. When we performed for the Library of Congress, our first show, there were sheets of paper all over the floor by my monitor."

"Noel is schooled as a musician," says Peter Rowan. "He knows jazz and pop music. If he wanted, he could go to a big city like L.A. or New York and be a session player. He's a real compadre. He still lives in South Texas. He takes that knowledge of everybody from Stevie Wonder to Herbie Hancock and funnels it into his part in the rhythm section of the Texmaniacs. He understands musical ideas quickly and can translate them for everybody else. In a sense, he's like a medical director. He has clear ideas of how something can be amplified musically to fulfill its potential."

It took us a long time to record again. Josh says, "We were just touring, trying to make ends meet. People were confused after David Farías left. They thought Los Texmaniacs had broken up, but we kept pushing until people knew what we were about."

We played some memorable shows. Fiddler David Greeley of Lafayette, Louisiana sat in with Los Texmaniacs one night. "I had no idea who he was," remembers Noel, "but he set up next to me and started playing. It jelled. It was like he had been playing with us for years."

Americano Groove was recorded at Sound Wave Studios in Tucson. We released it on my Line in the Sound label in June 2017. It included original songs—half in English and half in Spanish. When I write, I express things that happen to me, an experience, a true story. I try to make it catchy, something that will stick in your mind, but my songwriting is sporadic. It's hard for me to sit down and force myself to write. I could do it, but to me, a song has to come naturally. I'll get into a writing slump where I can't think. Then I'll clear my mind on an airplane or train and it'll open me up to creating lyrics.

The first song that I wrote was "Amor de Mi Vida (Love of My Life)." I was feeling good about the beautiful woman I was with. It's a serenade kind of song. It was a natural feeling I had in me.

It's best when I collaborate with somebody. Songs come out that much more special. I can come up with choruses and melodies—the hooks. It's the in-between stuff that I have difficulty with—the stories. On *Americano Groove*, I pretty much came up with the whole thing by myself. Alejandro Escobar helped with a couple of verses of "Down in the Barrio," singing about life where "bullets are flying, and people are dying." Joe Ely helped with the honky-tonk pickup tune "I Wanna Know Your Name." I sent him the lyrics and he tweaked them. We worked on them together. Augie Meyers played keyboards on "How Can a Beautiful Woman Be So Ugly." David Hidalgo of Los Lobos played a guitar solo on "Mentirosa." Kevin Fowler sang the bilingual Texas Tornado–like "Adios Mamacita." Rick Trevino sang "Big Night in a Small Town," a country tune that would have made Waylon Jennings and Merle Haggard smile. Tania Marie harmonized with me on a pop ballad, "How Long Is Patient," that would have fit snugly into the mid-1960s. Lorenzo Martínez sang "Herido." We played it at the 40th Anniversary concert of *A Prairie Home Companion*. "I'm glad Max is open to collaborating," says Noel. "It's about making a moment, creating a vibe. It doesn't have to be written down. There are rules to follow, but you can break them. That's what happens with Los Texmaniacs. We're open to letting anything happen."

Josh and I went back to the original instrumental bajo sexto/accordion sound for the polka "Muchachos Alegres." Other than "Polka Politos," which was my dad's polka, the instrumentals weren't original. They were old classics.

Steve Berlin produced *Americano Groove*. He says, "Once I got to know Max and the guys, it became automatic. Every time we were nearby, we'd play with each other. When they made their record, they reached out to me. Of course I was going to do it. We co-wrote a few songs and tried to expand the palette. I'm not sure what people expect from a Texmaniacs record, but we tried to make it varied and we happily succeeded."

"The album had traditional songs," says Noel, "but it also had other kinds of tunes. Max's approach to recording was what I'd always been about. We sat in the studio, at the same time, cutting it all at once. We didn't do a lot of editing. It was about capturing the moment, rather than a track. There's no magic in cutting tracks." Steve adds, "We experimented with different approaches, different styles. The studio itself was cool. It was a big open room. We could be in the same space and try different ideas. It was a positive experience."

It cost a lot of money to record *Americano Groove*, more than our budget.

We had nothing left for promotion and the album never got to radio stations or record shops. We had to do it the old way, selling them at our concerts.

Americano Groove was nominated for a Grammy, but the Recording Academy put it in the Americana category. We were up against the Mavericks, Brandi Carlile, Asleep at the Wheel, and Jason Isbell, who wound up winning the Grammy for his album *Something More Than Free*.

Radio stations were transitioning from albums and CDs to digital tracks. DJs used to play albums live in the studio. The same thing with CDs. Now, it's all digital downloads. When my dad recorded, there wasn't the technology of today. He recorded 45s and, before that, 78s. He'd take them directly to the radio stations and promote them. Back then, the stations had power. A lot of people listened to the radio. Narciso Martínez didn't have a television. He had a radio and heard German polkas through the airwaves.

I remember eight-track tapes and cassettes. When I first saw a CD, I was told that it was the future. CDs were thinner, less bulky, and had a cleaner sound. You could skip from one song to another immediately. But I miss liner notes.

I've played on so many records I can't count them all—over a hundred and fifty recordings. I recorded bluegrass on Charles Sawtelle's *Music from Rancho de Ville*. I've played on punk rock recordings. I've played on soundtracks, jazz albums. I recorded on two of Michelle Shocked's albums—*Mexican Standoff* and *Threesome*. Steve Berlin produced them. I played bass and bajo sexto.

I recorded on several of Willie J Laws' blues albums. I did a song on Michelle Martínez's album *Adrenaline*. I've played on country albums, traditional conjunto albums, hardcore South Texas conjunto albums. In the 1990s, I played on 90 percent of all of the Tejano albums that were popular. Most records that you heard on Tejano radio had me playing bajo sexto. I produced an album, *Tortilla Western Serenade*, for Tara Linda, in 2010. Flaco played on it, too. She describes her music as a mix of "Spaghetti Western, Tex-Mex, and rock."

Flaco and I recorded an album for Smithsonian Folkways, *Legends and Legacies*, in 2014. "We don't have to rehearse," Flaco says. "We know each other. It's really easy going. He's not pushing me but going with what I'm doing. It flows. Having fun and enjoying yourself." My desire had always been to record with just Flaco and me. When I brought the idea up, Flaco said, "Sure, what do you have in mind?" I talked to the Smithsonian about it. They asked about the concept. I told them that Flaco was the legend and I was the legacy. I wanted to do songs that Flaco used to play when he accompanied his father on bajo sexto and songs I played with my father.

Legends and Legacies was nominated for a Grammy. Flaco got a Grammy Lifetime Achievement Award, along with the Bee Gees, Pierre Boulez, Buddy Guy, George Harrison, the Isley Brothers, and Wayne Shorter. That made thirteen Grammy-winning albums I've participated on.

Flaco and I did the album live, straight up, with a conjunto. We used Flaco's son on drums and my bass player at the time, Óscar García. We just went into the studio and played songs we used to play with our fathers. It turned out to be a great album.

Los Texmaniacs released *Para la Raza* (2015) on our own. Josh played accordion. He says, "I worked on records with my uncle before I joined Los Texmaniacs. He'd produce someone and say, 'I've got an accordion player. My nephew could do it.' I was living upstairs from Max. He'd come up and ask me to do an accordion track. I'd make a little bit of cash. Working in the studio with him, I knew his way of thinking, the sound that he went for."

His father Jimmy, my brother, remembers that "Josh would record at the studio all the time, sometimes until two or three o'clock in the morning. He had school. His mother would get pissed off and tell me, 'Get him home early,' but we were busy. I'd get him home when I got him home. We had a couch

Max Baca, Lyle Lovett, and Noel Hernandez

in the studio. He would lie down and crash. Five thirty in the morning, I'd wake him and take him home. He'd fall asleep for a few more hours, get up, and go to school. He did the best he could, but all he cared about was music. His aunt bought him a dog. What do he think he named her? Música!"

A handful of Tejano artists came to the studio to sing with me. Roberto Pulido sang a song in his high, mellow style. His band, Roberto Pulido y Los Clasicos, has been called "the kings of beer-drinking ranchera music." Jimmy Edwards and David Marez sang with me. Flaco sang with me. David Farías sang with me.

"I sang harmony with my uncle on a conjunto standard," Josh remembers. "We were fishing for a vocal sound for Los Texmaniacs. Maybe because we're blood, there's a special connection. I'm not a dominant lead vocalist. Neither is my uncle. Doing it together, we had to step it up. I followed him and the harmonies came out pretty cool."

When I sang with my brother, he had a better voice, so I sang harmony. With David [Farías], he had the voice and I sang with him. After he left, I had to step it up. I'm not the greatest vocalist, but I can carry a tune. I do my best. I try to sing with feeling. Noel and Josh sing with me. They give me harmony. When Josh and I sing together, we sound like the Baca Brothers.

Josh's accordion playing also lifted things to another level. He has his own style—a very refreshing sound, but it's powerful, too. When he first came into the band, I told him that he had to listen to where this music came from. "It was always Flaco, Flaco, Flaco," Josh explains. "I listened to all of his records, and tried playing like him. I asked him who he had learned from and he told me about an accordionist from San Antonio, Manuel Guerrero, that he cohosted a radio show with in 1953, and Eugenio Abrego of Los Alegres de Terán, a Norteño duo formed in 1948 in Nuevo León, Mexico, about 130 miles from the border."

We recorded a mariachi tune and I asked Josh who should sing it. "I told him to forget about anyone else," Josh said. "'Do it yourself!' Who's ever heard Max Baca singing mariachi?"

A good friend, Eugene Rodríguez, invited Josh and me to his studio in Oakland, California, to collaborate with him and his group, Los Cenzontles (the Mockingbirds). We did some songs, but we didn't finish the album. Later on, Eugene asked Flaco and me to finish it. So half the album has Josh on the accordion, half has Flaco. Los Cenzontles is a great band. Lucina Rodríguez and Fabiola Trujillo sing beautifully together. The album was called *Carta Jugada*. Los Cenzontles Mexican Arts Center released it in 2017.

We recorded *Cruzando Borders*, our third Smithsonian Folkways album, at Ray Benson's Bismeaux Studio in Austin. He recently sold it. The new owners leveled it. Ours was one of the last albums to come out of the studio.

Josh says, "We went into the studio blind. We had no songs, no arrangements, nothing. The only time that I played the opening track, 'Mexico Americano,' was when I was helping Los Lobos out. We tried it and did one take. That's the take they kept. We pulled it out and played it." Noel reports, "I had to sing a lot on the album, doing backup for Max's lead. I sang on 80 percent of the songs. Some songs I'd heard all of my life. Some were fresh to me. I had to step it up and make it happen."

The original concept was to play narrative ballads or corridos. Daniel Sheehy called me and said, "With all this stuff about President Trump and the border wall happening now, it might be time to do an album about borders." "Max wanted to name it *Crossing the Border*," says Josh, "but I told him, 'No.' We take traditional instruments and cross them into the realm of folk music, bluegrass, and rock. We're crossing borders."

Lyle Lovett sang Woody Guthrie's song about migrant workers, "Deportee" (Plane Wreck at Los Gatos). Josh says, "I didn't know what to expect. We were in the studio, working on the song, trying to catch the vibe and energy. We went to D, then we went to E-flat. We worked on it while Lyle studied the lyrics. He didn't want to sing it the way that Los Super Seven recorded it on their Grammy-winning record with Max, Joe Ely, and Joel José Guzman. I had Joel's accordion playing in my brain. I learned the song in that position on the accordion, but they changed it to E-flat. I hate playing in that key. I said, 'I'm just going to do it like this.' I went in and cut a couple of takes. I was done. Lyle did his vocals. Lorenzo recorded his drums. We did it all first take. We nailed it. It's awesome hearing Lyle Lovett singing next to a bajo sexto and a button accordion.

"That night, we were hanging. It was enough for the day. We were burnt. We left and went to the hotel. A buddy of mine called me from Austin and said they were having a jam session at his bar. I told him, 'Okay, we'll swing by and get a nightcap.' Lorenzo, Noel, my uncle, and I took off for the bar. We were just going to have a drink. We had an early call in the morning. Noel had his own car. My uncle had a car. We went and played a couple of songs. Max didn't have his bajo sexto; he left it at the studio. He had to play guitar. Max left, but Lorenzo, Noel, and I stayed for the rest of the night. We got trashed. I know I did, for sure. I was rooming with Noel. 'Hey Josh, we've got to go.' 'Oh God!' I was buzzing. I had barely slept. We got to the studio and did 'I Am a Mexican,' the Rick Trevino composition. I was still spinning. We had a little tequila left so I took a couple of shots. I don't remember recording the song, but the vibe worked. It had a great groove. It's a beautiful song."

Cruzando Borders was nominated for a "Best Regional Mexican Performance" Grammy. It was an honor to be nominated, very humbling, but it was a tough category. We won the Grammy for *Borders y Bailes* in 2010 as the year's "Best Tejano Album." Two years later, the Recording Academy got rid of that category. They went from one hundred and nine Grammy categories to seventy-eight. Seven Latin categories were reduced to four. In our category was Mariachi Sol de Mexico, one of the biggest bands in the history of Mariachi music, Ángela Aguilar, Aida Cuevas, and Calibre 50. Luis Miguel won the Grammy for *¡Mexico Por Siempre!*

Noel says, "The awards ceremony was very exciting, the whole energy of it. It was something fresh for me, I had never been there before. My previous band, Los Frijoles Románticos, had been nominated, but I hadn't been able to go to the ceremony. I had other commitments. When *Cruzando Borders* was nominated, I didn't think I was going to go. Max and Josh were going. Max called me and said, 'Hey man, I want you to come with us. You're part of this band.' I was cool about not going. It's expensive to get there, but Max made it happen. It was a ball. I was glad to see Buddy Guy get recognition. They announced his award before our category. We didn't get the Grammy but being nominated was a big honor."

"We were pulling teeth that whole year," adds Josh, "gigging and traveling. We were pounding our music, and who we are, into people's faces. We did lots of house concerts and festivals. We'd travel if we could play a house concert. We just kept on traveling, making ends meet. We went to California to play a house concert for a friend. It was an all-acoustic concert. There was zero electricity. The morning before our show, I heard my uncle saying, 'Josh, Josh.' I walked to the back of the house, where he was, and he said, 'We've been nominated!' After that, my phone went crazy, my Facebook, instant messenger. We were getting calls from everybody, congratulating us. We were on cloud nine. It was such a beautiful feeling. We were nominated for a record where we just went in and played like kids. Of course, we did it correctly, but it came from love, friendship, family, blood, and all that hard work. My uncle has done so much for me, as far as opening doors, but I've got to cut the mustard."

Josh went home and told his wife about the nomination: "I was so excited. I got our tickets for the awards ceremony and we went shopping for what we were going to wear. The whole band went with our partners. We looked for gigs we could do while we were in California. It was an amazing experience. I'm just a Mexican American kid who grew up in the barrio, but I got to shake the hand of Buddy Guy. He said, 'I remember you guys.' We played at the Vancouver Island Festival together. He remembered. Then later, I went to the party—free food and tequila, hanging and chilling. It was a great feeling to know that all the hard work had paid off. Those people were there to recognize what we had done. The stars aligned."

FIFTEEN

CANTANDO POR UNA CAUSA
(Singing for a Cause)

I feel blessed when I look at where I've been: Bosnia, Kosovo, Macedonia, Serbia, Iraq, Kyrgyzstan, Afghanistan, China, Russia, Mongolia, Bangladesh, South America—Brazil, Argentina—all through Europe—Spain, Holland, Switzerland, Germany, Austria, Sweden, and Finland. I've gotten to experience different cultures. My musical journey has allowed me to listen to an oud here, an Appalachian fiddle there, the different ways people sing, exercising their culture and their feelings. I've heard Mongolian throat singers, gone to Iraq and heard people chanting. It's opened my mind. The main cause of racism is that people are not educated enough to see that there're beautiful people around the world.

During our first trip, we went to Iraq through MWR (Military Warfare Recreation) and played for the troops. A war was going on. Toby Keith went to play for the troops around the same time, but he went for the USO and played at bigger bases.

"One of our first gigs, Max told me about it," David Farías recalls, "and I asked him where it was. He told me Iraq. What!? Is there an Iraq in Texas? It was an experience. You see a lot on TV, but being there is unforgettable. People thanked us for being there. We thanked them for the service they're doing for us. One day we played for a hundred people, the next day a thousand people, and the day after that more. Our job was to entertain the troops."

Our first gig in Iraq was in Kirkuk on New Year's Eve 2005–2006. Lorenzo Martínez says, "We were so exhausted from jet lag, we had no worries."

I freaked out when we met some Iraqi soldiers. We had heard so much about the war, I didn't understand why we'd be playing for Iraqi soldiers. It turned out they were actually on our side. We took a photograph with them.

We were constantly being mortar-bombed, two or three times a day. We signed our lives away when we accepted the invitation. They flew us in two Blackhawks. They took seats out to make a place for our instruments, PA system, and drums on one and we flew in the other.

We met our tour guide in California before we left. Sergeants were always traveling with us. They had big rifles they held outside the windows of the Blackhawks. I never dreamt of playing music during a war.

I remember the first time we had an incoming missile. We were onstage in Kirkuk, playing in a big tent for about two hundred soldiers, men and women. They were dancing and having a good time. We didn't hear the sirens signaling incoming FOB [fractional orbital bombardment] missiles. When the sirens go off, you've got ten to fifteen seconds to get to a bunker. All of a sudden, a missile hit about a hundred yards from the tent. We felt the stage shake and the tent suck in. It was like an earthquake. We dropped our instruments, put our bulletproof vests and helmets on, and ran to the bunker.

"The soldiers started running to their positions," recalls Lorenzo. "I had a helmet right by my drums. I put it on."

Iraq, 2005

David remembers, "We were doing what we loved doing, jamming out and, all of a sudden, we saw the tent caving in. We could hear the missile, like a whistle. We heard a pop and then the sirens. We got off the stage, put our helmets on, and ran to the bunkers. We weren't scared. We were there to play the songs."

If there's one missile, there's usually another. We were sitting in the bunker, lights out. It was completely dark and quiet. You couldn't hear anyone talking. There were soldiers on either side of us with their guns out, protecting us. I was thinking that we were going to get killed. During the orientation before we agreed to go, they told us what it was going to be like, but I had no clue until I was actually there. We heard another explosion and the ground shook. Then it got quiet. We heard someone on the radio say, "All clear." The sergeant turned around and told us, "Okay, guys, follow me."

That second explosion turned out to be the US Army retaliating. Everything for a mile radius of where the enemy missile had originated was totally destroyed. Afterward, they took us back to the stage and told us to play. I didn't feel like playing—I was so scared—but to the soldiers, it was no big deal. It was their everyday routine.

There were times when we'd be eating lunch with the soldiers and sirens would go off. We'd get up, grab our vests and helmets, and hustle to the bunkers. There were bunkers everywhere.

We flew into a place called Tent City. As far as your eye could see, there were tents. We flew in at three in the morning. They put us up in a big tent, fifteen soldiers to a tent. They gave us cots and sleeping bags. Even though we were there to entertain and play music, we were hanging out with the soldiers. It was like being in the Army.

Marines travel at night. We would sometimes go with them in Chinooks. We'd sit on benches, look out the windows, and see tracer bullets being shot at us. They looked like fireworks. It was Iraqis firing at us, but they couldn't exactly see where we were. They didn't have the infrared technology that the Marines had, so they were guessing and shooting. I asked one of the soldiers protecting us if we could be hit and he said, "Yeah, guard your ass."

From Kirkuk, we went to Ramadi, the capitol of Iraq's Anbar Province. That's where Saddam Hussein had his palace. We flew in under sniper attack, so we couldn't play. We could perform in orange and yellow zones, but this was in the red zone. They put us in a safe spot overnight. The next day, we had to fly out and go somewhere in the yellow zone to entertain the troops. They got us up at six in the morning and gave us ten minutes to get ready—shower and everything. We were supposed to go by Blackhawk, but they needed the Blackhawks because they were under attack. They took the two Blackhawks we were supposed to go in and told us that we were going to get on a convoy to Al-Ramadi, where they had just blown up Saddam's sons' palaces. These huge palaces were smoldering. We had to go about five miles, right through the city. It was scary. Our instruments were in the big truck behind us. There were two musicians in one Hummer, with a gunner and a driver, and the other two were in another Hummer, with a gunner and driver. The Blackhawks that were supposed to be ours fell. They had flown out and gotten bombed. My heart dropped, but things happen for a reason. It wasn't our time. It would have been us in those Blackhawks.

It was over 120 degrees. It was so hot, you didn't sweat. The heat would dry your sweat. We got dehydrated very quickly and had to have bottled water constantly. We had two bottles with us all the time. I threw up because it was so hot. We smelled oil and gas fumes. We did it because it was our duty to the soldiers.

The Marines took us to Saddam Hussein's palace. They wouldn't let us take pictures, but I asked if we could look inside. They took us through the front door. Everything was gold, even the toilet seat. There was gold on the walls. They let us look for five minutes before escorting us out.

In the red zone, they'd take us to medical facilities and we'd play for the wounded. Even if we didn't play, just talking to them helped. They told us about their experiences, what they had seen. Anything we could do to take their minds off their problems was good. We talked to soldiers when they were eating lunch or dinner. A lot of them were from Texas, Arizona, New Mexico, and California.

"There's no alcohol on certain bases," says Lorenzo, "so they drink alcohol-free beer. That was disappointing. We drank a couple to be cordial."

A year later, we went to Afghanistan, where all the action was happening. It was much more dangerous. We had a couple of close calls. We flew on a Cessna C-120, this huge airplane used for transporting tanks.

There were Russian land mines on one base. From time to time, they'd go off; they'd been there for years. They gave us a tour of the perimeter of the base. We saw nonmilitary volunteer workers in front-end loaders digging up the ground where these land mines were to get rid of them. Sometimes they'd go off. That was the whole idea. They wanted to get rid of these land mines. Little kids would run up to the fence and soldiers would give them candy bars. Kids were playing in the dirt near the land mines. God forbid one of those land mines went off.

We performed for the soldiers. We were supposed to fly out the next day, but we got stranded for three days. There was a sandstorm and the Chinooks we were supposed to go back in couldn't fly. There wasn't much to do except eat three times a day. One day, we were eating lunch and BOOM! Sirens went off and we ran to the bunkers. It was intense.

We toured Bosnia-Herzegovina, Serbia, the Balkans, Macedonia, and Kosovo the following year. Once in a while, there'd be an incoming missile, but there was no war; it was a lot more relaxed.

When we returned to Iraq in 2009, we slept in what the Bible calls the Garden of Eden. The Jordan River went through it, but it was dry; there was no water. We went to the city of Ur, in northern Iraq, and saw where Abraham was born.

A few American soldiers committed suicide while we were there. They went to the latrine and killed themselves. It was pretty sad.

We had to wait to use one of two phones to call home. We were given PX money to spend in the base's store. After that first bombing, I went into the PX and bought new underwear.

I saw one soldier with his head down, crying. I don't know what had happened, but he was depressed. I spoke to him and told him things would be all right. Meeting soldiers and talking to them, seeing them with their limbs blown off in the medical facilities, hearing about their experiences on the battlefield, opens your eyes and humbles you, brings you down to Earth. You come home and hear about gangs and Mexican cartels killing people. They may be bad-asses, but I'd like to see them go to Iraq and see how bad-ass they could be.

Soldiers would walk up to the stage to watch us play. Tears of joy would come out of their eyes or they'd smile with so much laughter. We played Texas music—"San Antonio Rose" and "El Paso"—and Cajun tunes and they'd be reminded of their hometowns and culture. After we played, we'd speak to soldiers and sign autographs. They were so excited that we were there. It took their minds off their situation and lifted their spirits. They loved it. I'd do it again.

China, 2010

Not all of our travels have been to war zones. "We got to play in China twice," says Noel, "for people who had never heard this genre of music before. They grew up differently than how we grew up. They lived in a Communist country. To them, we were the American West. They were eager to listen. When Josh played a polka, they clapped, but they had no idea how they were supposed to dance. They started to move, and I saw security trying to calm them down. It was strict, a whole other world, but it touched my heart that we could move them so much with our music. Music gives a sense of freedom, a sense of liberty. There are no borders in music; it's universal."

China is a Communist country and the government blocks things they don't want people to be exposed to. They're limited to what they can see or hear. We were driving on the highway in Beijing when, all of a sudden, we saw a billboard of us holding our Grammy awards. We had to send in our set list before our shows. We translated our Spanish songs into English and sent it to them. They translated the words into Chinese and projected them onto screens on either side of the stage so people could tell what we were singing.

"At the end of our show," Josh remembers, "people came up to us crying. I asked one of them what was the matter. Through our tour guide, she told us that our song had touched her heart. She had been trying to move her parents into China from another country. The border wouldn't allow them to cross, even though there would be a better life for them. This goes on all over the world. It's not just happening between Mexico and Texas. It's happening between Canada and America, Colorado and California, everywhere. People are trying to cross a border, cross that path in their life, better themselves or get away from something they're running from, a heartache, or running towards like love, passion, something they're striving for. I respect the people crossing the border. My mom's parents lived in this country until passing away in 1974. They crossed the border and strove, struggled, and worked. I grew up with a big American flag in my front yard. My grandfather was a World War II veteran, my great-grandfather was a World War I veteran. Uncle Carl was a Vietnam vet. I have cousins fighting in Iraq. I'm more American than anyone can possibly be. We didn't cross the border. The border crossed us."

You have to be invited to perform in Communist countries. We had to get invitations from China, Bangladesh, and Russia. We played concerts through the US Consulates. They took us to beautiful four-to-five-thousand-seat theaters. We played the Philharmonic Hall in Moscow, beautiful cathedrals in St. Petersburg. There was all that history.

We played a country music festival in India, close to where it meets China—the Mongolian region. It wasn't Garth Brooks kind of country or what we think of as country music, but music from different countries. We represented music from the United States.

During our second trip to Russia, we played festivals. We traveled on an overnight train. The next night, we'd be on the other side of Russia. We'd do the gig and get back on the train. Russia is huge.

Spain was very cool. People already knew our music before we got there. They associated me with Flaco because I toured so many years with him. Flaco is huge in Spain.

We were touring China when our guides told us, "You've got three days before your next concert. You could stay in your hotel or go to an Indigenous village and do community outreach." That's what we did. We drove six hours south of Beijing and then another two hours into the mountains until we came to a village of two hundred people. It was just like you'd see in *National Geographic*. People walked up these mountains to pick their vegetables in the morning. They carried them on bamboo sticks. That was what they were going to eat that day. There were no convenience stores, no paved roads, but they had a small cultural center.

I met Ping Xu in China and we became pen pals. She loves music. The Chinese are not allowed to have Facebook, YouTube, or Google, so we communicated with each other through email. We did that for a while. Around 2017, she got in touch with me. She had moved to New York. We talked more and I got her phone number. She told me that she'd be coming to San Antonio for two weeks. When she came down, we went to dinner.

Her spirit is so beautiful. She doesn't have a bad bone in her. She told me, after we started dating, "I'll be honest with you. I liked you because of your music, but I didn't want to date you. You've won my heart over."

Max Baca and Ping Xu, 2020

I hadn't been looking for romance. I was getting out of a relationship. Ping and I were friends. We'd go out to dinner, but as time went on, we started getting more intimate and into a relationship. She moved in with me. I said, "This is the one."

All my life, I had been chasing women, trying to make them happy, trying to impress them, trying to win them over. It was always me catering to them. For the first time in my life, it was the opposite. I had finally met somebody who took care of me genuinely from the heart.

She's learning English. Thank God for Google Translator. I wasn't educated enough. I'll say something on Google Translator, and it'll come out slang. She won't be able to understand it. She'll answer back and it'll come out intelligently. She's very smart.

Ping has been away from China for four years. She hasn't seen her fifteen-year-old son in all that time. She talks to him via Skype every day. She hopes to bring him to the USA to go to college. He's going to start the ninth grade. Last year, her father passed away. She wasn't able to go back to China.

After we got married, we started working on getting her green card and citizenship. I promised to take her to China so she could visit the cemetery where her dad is buried. That's what she really wants. She needs the closure.

She cries at night sometimes. I'll wake up and she'll be sobbing. She cries herself to sleep sometimes. She'll turn to me and tell me that she loves me. She really means it. I'm very blessed to have her.

In China, couples are only allowed to have two children. Ping freaked out when she saw how big our families are. Josh and his wife have six kids—triplets and twins from her previous relationship and a little girl.

We visited my family in Albuquerque. On the way home, Ping started crying. I asked her why. She told me, "Because I'm happy. I have a family now."

Our wedding was simple. We got up one day. She said, "What do you want to do today?" I said, "Let's get married." "Okay." We went to the courthouse, signed the papers, went to the next level where they had a judge, and got married. That was it. I went in shorts. To me, it's not about cakes, flowers, or spending money to entertain people. It's like Christmas. It's not about presents and Santa Claus. I've been married twice before, with celebrations, hiring a band, buying dresses, tuxedos, rehearsing how to walk into a room. That's not what it's about. It should be about two people in love. Let's commit, not to everybody else, but to the two of us. Use that money to better your life together.

"I'm so happy that Donny met this girl," says my mother. "I just love her. She's adorable. She takes good care of him. They're happy. As a mother, I feel that God answered my prayers."

Traveling and being away from home hasn't always been easy. Josh says, "It's tough being a dad and a husband. I've gone on tour and when I get home, my son is already as big as me. What happened? He's not a kid anymore. He's a man. My daughter is already talking like she's smart; she is. She's going to school. Being home and teaching my kids, coaching their baseball team, is incredible. I missed my daughter's graduation ceremony. She made all-A's honor roll in advanced classes. My son just got his first job. My wife is there by herself, cooking and cleaning, picking this one up from football, this one from basketball, taking that one to work, taking my daughter to school. It takes its toll on your heart and your mind. I need to be there, but I need to work. I've got to keep the lights on and the grass cut. They need food and clothes."

"We've had a lot of great times traveling," says Lorenzo, "sharing like family, but it's a struggle to be away. I teach Americana guitar and music theory at a Los Angeles County jail and help take care of my mother. She's going to be ninety-five next week. I'm blessed to still have her. Max's mother is elderly, as well. Our fathers passed too early, I believe. They were both World War II veterans. My father was in the Battle of the Bulge. Max and I have shared stories about our fathers. Music kept them going forward."

"My father loved music," he continues, "and fiddled a little with the guitar, but I mainly get it from my mama—Francisca Martínez's side. She studied music but married early and her schooling ended." Despite the distance between Los Angeles and San Antonio, Lorenzo says, "I can't give Los Tex-maniacs up. I'm part of the evolution of the group. Regardless of who's sitting in for me, I know my place is always there."

Cantando por una Causa (Singing for a Cause)

SIXTEEN

CARLOS

My son, Carlos Baca, was born on February 8, 1985. I had just left the lumberyard job. His mother told me, "You're not making enough money at the lumberyard. You need a better job," so I took a job as a scaler for a construction company. I made $2.35 an hour and worked twenty hours a week. I'd be lucky if I made fifty bucks after taxes, but I liked the owner, Mr. Sandoval. His son, Michael, and I became friends. In middle school, he was always in trouble. His seat was in the corner all the time.

For most of Carlos's childhood, I was on the road with the Texas Tornados and gone for weeks at a time. I couldn't be there like a normal father, taking him to baseball games and picking him up from school. I was gone, living from hotel to hotel. When I wasn't playing with the Texas Tornados, I was playing with Flaco. From the age of twenty-three, I might be home once a month for two or three days. My son was either with his mother or my mother. I didn't have much time to spend with him, but when he was born, I was the happiest guy in the world. I was there and saw him being born. It was amazing. I helped the doctor clean him, fresh out of the oven. They wrapped him in blankets and the doctor gave him to me to hold: "Here's your son." When I held him, I was instantly in love.

His mother and I were young. I was eighteen. She was seventeen. It was a child having a child. I don't regret having a son, but his mother and I didn't get along at times. We fought a lot. That led to a separation. There were times when she kept him from me and didn't let me see him. She was mad at me. That would hurt me. There was one time I'll never forget. I was in my room. She took my son and said, "You're never going to see him again." I was so

Max Baca and Carlos Baca, 1987

young, I believed her. I didn't know any better. I remember lying on my bed, sobbing, missing my son. I hadn't seen him in a couple of weeks. My mom came in my room and sat next to me. She wiped my tears. In a genuinely soft voice, she said, "You love your son?" I said, "Yes, I do." She said, "Don't worry, you're going to see him again. Time heals all wounds." I felt the strongest love you could imagine when she told me that. It gave me a new breath of life. She was right.

My son got to the point where he wanted to be with me, but I couldn't do it. I was on the road working. People tell me to stop beating myself up, but I was a coward. I couldn't stop playing music and just raise my son. It's what his mother wanted. She gave me an ultimatum. She said, "It's either me or your music." I said, "Well, I'll see you. I love my music too much."

My dad told me a long time ago, "Son, there's a difference between having a baby and getting married. Just because you're having a baby, it doesn't mean you have to get married." Those were words of wisdom from my dad, but he wanted me to do the right things. I married my son's mom and tried to be a father, but it was my destiny to play music. I don't know anything else.

"I remember going to the smaller gigs that my dad and my uncle had," Carlos says from Albuquerque, "at church fiestas and parties—my cousins and me. It was pretty amazing to see my dad traveling with the Texas Tornados, forming his own group and winning a Grammy. It was significant, pretty awesome. I loved the music. It was very comforting. Whenever I hear conjunto music, it takes me back to my childhood. It gives me a sense of home and comfort."

Carlos was a baby when he met Flaco. "He's like a grandfather," he says. "I've known him my entire life—a major, world-known superstar. It's never crossed my mind of him as being anything other than humble. Óscar Téllez would come every so often and stay for a couple of months," he continues. "He'd sleep in the garage, hang out, and play music. He was a jokester, hilarious. He'd tell jokes and he'd do magic tricks and card tricks. He was great."

When my son was in middle school, I told him, "Come, let's go get a bite to eat." We sat down and ate. Afterward, I took him to an ice cream store. My dad used to do that to me. He wasn't the type to say, "Son, give me a hug." He would never do that. He was military. His way of saying "I love you" was buying an ice cream cone. He'd never eat but watched me eat. I thought that was the way I was supposed to be. I was hard and cold, too. It was confusing. Inside me, my heart is like my mom's. She was the one who hugged us. My brain is like my dad's. For some reason, my heart outweighs my brain. I was always thinking with my heart until I couldn't take things anymore. Then my brain would kick in and I'd be Mr. Tough Guy.

I told my son that I wanted to apologize for being a coward and not being there for him. He stopped me and said, "I forgave you a long time ago." That was a new start for our relationship.

He's made me a grandpa. I have two grandchildren—a thirteen-year-old grandson, Carlitos Max Baca, and a ten-year-old granddaughter, Mya Jole Baca. I always wanted a little girl. She's the love of my life and she loves her grandpa.

My son and his wife stayed with me when my granddaughter was born. I watched her and her brother during the week, while they went to work. We got really attached. In the morning, I'd hear my granddaughter coming from the bedroom, little footsteps running down the hallway. She'd open my door slowly. She'd come in and walk over to my bed. She wouldn't say, "Wake up, grandpa." She'd just look right at me. I would stay quiet and see what she was going to say. You love your children, but grandchildren are a different kind of love. They're your blood from your child.

My grandson is taking guitar in school. He's into theatre. I've been to some of his plays during the holidays. He's incredibly talented. He and my granddaughter can sing. They have good voices.

My son doesn't play music. When he was a baby, he would hear me practicing the bajo sexto or the drums, but he never took a liking to playing music. He likes listening to it, but not playing. He never had it in him to do it. ("My grandfather had the tax business," Carlos explains, "and I gravitated more to that.")

My son is highly intelligent. His mother is very smart, but his dad only went to the tenth grade. I had to repeat it and repeat it. I never got enough credits. I missed so much school because I was playing music. It was hard to catch up, but I was nine years old, making $150 a week playing music. For a kid, that's rather good.

I'm humbled when someone tells me how much I've influenced them. A bajo sexto player from Arizona, Stevie Ray Vavages, has been staying in a room in my house and playing music around San Antonio. He's a full-blooded Tohono O'odham Indian. His father and uncle had a waila band on the reservation. "My dad played guitar," he said while driving to the Alamo. "My uncle pulled me aside and gave me an acoustic guitar with four strings. He said, 'You're going to play this.' I was excited because I was like my cousins who wanted to play with their uncles. Our uncles were the coolest people in the world. Within a month, I had my first gig. I was thirteen. I thought my uncle was teaching me guitar, but later on, I realized that he was teaching me bajo sexto chords. I just went on from there. Our bass player played bajo sexto. He taught me a little more and I learned from other musicians by listening and emulating. I drifted into Norteño, Tejano, and conjunto music and fell in love with it."

Stevie and I met about ten years ago. "Los Texmaniacs were playing in Arizona," he remembers. "I was a big fan. The chairman of the Pascua Yaqui Reservation also plays bajo sexto and he knows me. He saw me in the crowd and gave me the heads-up to come backstage. As soon as I got back there, he said, 'Have fun!' Max was about to go on stage. I was excited to meet him. We spoke for a minute and he told me to come back later. That started our friendship."

SEVENTEEN

¿ADÓNDE VAMOS DESDE AQUÍ?
(Where Do We Go from Here?)

Los Texmaniacs is preparing another folkloric album for Smithsonian Folkways, but we're also working on an original album. Josh and I are writing the songs. He's a great songwriter. He's got a lot of stories. It takes talent to write songs; you've got to be open-minded.

"We're creating a new repertoire," says Josh. "We've gotten more educated, musically, by playing with other artists, hearing a lick that's cool and adapting it. It's a different energy, but it's true to the art and music."

Over the years, I've kept up with what Peter Rowan was doing. We'd run into each other backstage or at a festival. Los Texmaniacs was invited to play the 2006 Richmond Folklife Festival in Richmond, Virginia. Peter was invited, too. He asked if he could sit in with us.

"Max was like, 'Hey man, let's play,'" Peter remembers. "I thought, 'Wow! This is a whole new generation.'" I'd heard Flaco's band call him out for playing with Caucasians, right in front of me. There was a movement called 'La Raza' in the Southwest Latino culture in the late '60s. Their race was endangered and persecuted. The Hispanic were considered the low life, but they didn't feel that way about themselves. The movement said, 'Let's raise up our people.' That complicated things for traditionalists that played with Flaco. They were like, 'You're not sticking with your own people.' Flaco received a lot of flak for being inclusive, but the spirit was inclusiveness, not because of race, but based on music. There are so many similarities between what they call Tex-Mex and what they call bluegrass. I don't think those two styles combine well, but elements from both do."

By the time we met again, according to Peter, "the attitude of the whole La

Peter Rowan and Max Baca.

143

¿Adónde Vamos desde Aquí? (Where Do We Go from Here?)

Raza thing, the older generation fear of an endangered culture had changed." He explains, "Max never felt that his culture was endangered. He just felt the honor of being a lineage holder who could bring it forth. When we met in Virginia, I was trying to live up to the promise that bluegrass made to me and I made to it—to fulfill my heritage in bluegrass from the Bill Monroe years. I had a quartet. We were doing fine. We had a good run because it was my first bluegrass band of my own—Jody Stecher, Keith Little, and Paul Knight. We didn't even have a fiddle player. And there was Max. He had a group with him. We played together. Max was so enthusiastic. He was the same kid—'C'mon, let's play.'"

I've always considered Peter to be part of the tradition because of what he did with Flaco, but "Nobody in the bluegrass world gave a damn that I played with Flaco," he claims. "No critic said anything good about it, yet it was based on love and music."

Two or three years ago, I called Peter. He remembers, "Max and I had been in touch over the years. He told me, 'Let's do a Christmas tour.' I thought, 'That's ambitious.' Seeing how hard he worked to make things happen was a surprise. I agreed to do a few dates. I went to Texas and they treated me well. Flaco was there. It was great."

A year ago, Peter called and asked if we could come to MerleFest in North Carolina. "MerleFest offered me two shows," he explains, "one with my blue-grass band and one with something called the Free Mexican Airforce. Max and Josh flew over to play the Sunday set with me. The response was so good that it created interest with the people who book me. Instead of waiting for offers for bluegrass, which became less and less, it was time for something different. I'm the one who invented the eclecticism of Peter Rowan by going to Jamaica, Hawaii, and India, playing Texas music. It was a time of mixing. What we're doing now is the fruition of the seeds that were planted then."

Peter Rowan and Los Texmaniacs have continued to work together. Peter says, "All this year's big gigs are with Los Texmaniacs: Telluride, MerleFest, and Spring Fest at the Suwanee. We played in New Orleans. We've been together a long time already, just with the shows we've played. They knew all of my songs already, the ones I did with Flaco. I wish we had toured more. It's a late career thing, but in a way, it's full circle. It can develop into something great."

Playing with Flaco's bajo sexto player, Jesse Ponce, Peter learned his rhythm on the guitar. With Los Texmaniacs, we take care of that. "It leaves me free to be a singer," Peter says. "I don't have to worry about playing rhythm guitar. There's plenty of rhythm in Los Texmaniacs. I can float on top with more ornamental, sustaining, electric guitar playing. I'm always trying to find a way to put a song over. Los Texmaniacs are so supportive, I can find that place. Max is always there, on my right side, laying it in.

"It's about being responsive to environment, language, and food. When you go someplace and eat the food that the people eat, hear the sounds they hear, and immerse in their language as much as possible, you have a sense of empathy for the vastness of human beings in this world. As a Buddhist, that means ultimately enlightenment. Freedom is the underlining theme of what I'm trying to do, take the roots and run with them. I owe that to Tex Logan, Joe Val, Don Stover, Bill Monroe, people who saw that I wasn't a dilettante but someone deeply connecting with the music."

Working with Peter has been a learning experience for the whole band. Noel says, "Backing him on his great hits is an honor, but my favorite thing is just hanging with him and hearing him talk. If you catch on to what he

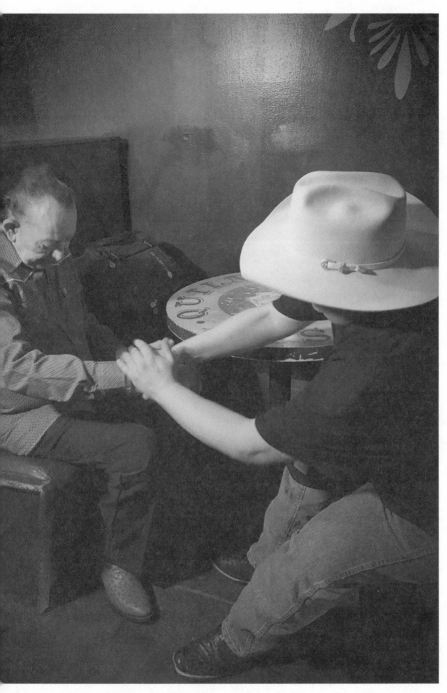

Flaco Jiménez and Max Baca, 2020

says, you learn so much. He's a great artist, a great writer. We can get loud as Los Texmaniacs. We can hit it hard and give it power, but when we play with Peter, we have to go the other way. We bring the dynamics lower. I'll barely hit the strings of my bass, but I'm creating the foundation. It feels so good. Peter's beautiful voice dictates, for all of us, where to go."

When you're writing a song, you can get stuck. I've been trying to finish one song since the early '90s. It's called "Imaginary Mind." I showed it to Peter, and he liked it. We've been finishing it together.

We've learned a lot of Peter's bluegrass songs, like "Old Santa Fe." Peter says, "I want to do an epic version of 'Wild Mustang,' which I recorded with Tony Rice in 2004. It's going to be a big sound. We also have that sweet spot with drum, bass, bajo sexto, accordion, and acoustic guitar. We need to develop that." He calls these new songs "anthemic, a little more power-to-the-people kind of music. It's material I've written over the years. There was never a place for it. Jerry Douglas loves one of the songs, 'Mississippi California,' about a border guard. I sang it for Flaco when he came to Nashville. It's the perfect tune. The time has come. As my friend Chris Henry, the great bluegrass mandolin player, says, it's what the spirit wants. That's a funny concept that there's a spirit in the world that wants us to bring forth these good things, but it's not a coincidence or commerciality."

Before touring with Peter, Josh brought his accordions to Flaco to be repaired, cleaned, and prepared for the road. "I told him I was going to be playing with Peter," Josh recalls, "and he told me to play Peter's song 'Break My Heart Again.' I played it and he said, 'That was good, but try it like this.' He showed me exactly how he recorded it. On stage in San Francisco, I played it like he showed me. I looked to my left and saw Peter looking at me. I was in the spot where Flaco was when he was my age—playing with Peter and doing the same song. My accordion is set up exactly like Flaco's: the way the buttons are set up, the action, the thumb strap, and the tuning are identical. It was meant to be."

At first, Josh wasn't familiar with Peter Rowan: "I asked my uncle who he was, and he assured me that he was a cool dude. The first time we played together, my uncle told me the wrong key for the song, so I brought the wrong accordion to the rehearsal. I'm able to play all the keys on my box, so I pulled it out as much as I could. Peter liked it."

In January 2020, we recorded two tracks with Peter in Joel Savoy's studio in Eunice, Louisiana. Joel's dad, Marc Savoy, is a Cajun accordion maker. "They all knew Max," says Peter. "The connection between Tex-Mex and Cajun musicians has grown over the years."

We recorded a rhumba, "Down South in New Orleans," written by Jack and Jim Anglin and Johnny Wright and done originally by Johnny and Jack in 1953, and a new tune, "Alligator Alley." Peter explains, "It's about this moonshiner. The law is hunting him, but he hides in Alligator Alley. It's a rocker. I'm heading towards the ultimate Tex-Mex twang music."

Peter wrote a song that we're going to record, "Ain't No Telling." "It's a ragtime tune with a minor section," he says, "very New Orleans sounding. We went through it on stage. People thought it was a traditional tune, but I was making it up on the spot. Josh brought in this Parisian accordion sound. Oh my God! Where did that come from? He said, 'I hit a switch.' It's an acoustic instrument, but there are a couple of levers you use to rearrange to change the sound. I'd like to hear him play the piano. I bet it would be amazing. I love being between Max and Josh onstage."

In July 2019, we participated in a Vancouver Island Festival workshop celebrating the fiftieth anniversary of the Woodstock Music Festival. Josh recalls, "We played Creedence Clearwater Revival's 'Born on the Bayou' with bajo sexto and accordion, and added a Spanish verse. Instead of singing 'I can still hear my old hound dog barkin', we sang 'I can hear my chihuahua barking.' It was more on the Chicano side of things. I did the *Josh Baca Experience*, adding pedals and playing Jimi Hendrix's 'Purple Haze' on the accordion instead of the guitar. Then I did 'Fire' by Jimi Hendrix. I also sang 'Bad Moon Rising' by Creedence Clearwater Revival. We did it Tex-Mex style."

Those songs became part of our repertoire. "We've been playing them all over the place," says Josh, "improvising, and having fun. It's refreshing to get out of the box. We bring a different set list to every show. It keeps us from being monotonous. We've got hundreds of songs."

Max Baca

I'm humbled that the Conjunto Hall of Fame and the Tejano Music Hall of Fame inducted me. I've received a Lifetime Achievement Award from the state of New Mexico and proclamations from mayors and city councils. The mayor of San Antonio and the New Mexico Legislature awarded me proclamations as an ambassador of good will. Los Texmaniacs received awards and medals from every military installation where we performed.

I keep the "Best Tejano Album" Grammy for *Borders y Bailes* in a cabinet. Next to it, there's a letter from a second-grader. He wrote, "Dear Los Texmaniacs, we're doing a project in school thanking people for doing something for someone else. I chose you. I want to thank you for your beautiful music."

That letter means more to me than the Grammy. It's what it's all about.

Carlos Baca: February 25, 2020

Gloria Baca: February 25, 2020

Jimmy Baca: January 31, 2020

Josh Baca: February 25, 2020

Max Baca: December 4, 2019 to May 5, 2020

Steve Berlin: March 4, 2020

Eduardo Díaz: November 7, 2019

David Farías: February 26, 2020

Noel Hernández: January 24, 2020

Kathleen Hudson: November 8, 2020

Pat Jasper: November 7, 2019

Flaco Jiménez: February 25, 2020

Lorenzo Martínez: February 4, 2020

Augie Meyers: January 7, 2020

Gilbert Reyes: March 4, 2020

Peter Rowan: February 12, 2020

Daniel Sheehy: November 3, 2019

Juan Tejeda: October 31, 2019

Joe Treviño: March 10, 2020

Rick Trevino: February 26, 2020

Steve Vavages: February 26, 2020

LOS HERMANOS BACA

Mi Primer Amor (My First Love) (Max Baca Records, 1982)
Hey Baby (Qué Pasó) (Max Baca Records, 1985)
Squeeze It (Alva Vista, 1988)
Quiero Que Sepas (I Want You to Know) (Discos Joey, 1991)

FLACO JIMÉNEZ
(not including CDs released independently)

Flaco Jiménez (Arista, 1994)*
Buena Suerte, Señorita (Arista, 1996)
Said and Done (Virgin, 1998)*
Sleepytown (Back Porch, 2002)
Squeeze Box King (Compadre, 2003)
Flaco & Max: Legends and Legacies (Smithsonian Folkways, 2014)

TEXAS TORNADOS

4 Aces (Reprise, 1996)
Live from the Limo, vol. 1 (Virgin, 1999)
Live from Austin, TX (New West, 2005)

LOS SUPER SEVEN

Los Super Seven (RCA Nashville, 1998)*
Heard It on the X (RCA Nashville, 2005)

THE ROLLING STONES

Voodoo Lounge (Rolling Stones, 1994)

LOS TEXMANIACS

A Tex-Mex Groove (Maniax, 2004)
A Blue Cat Christmas (Tarantula, 2004)
About Time (Maniax, 2006)
Borders y Bailes (Smithsonian Folkways, 2009)*
Live in Texas (Maniax, 2012)
Texas Towns & Tex-Mex Sounds (Smithsonian Folkways, 2012)
Americano Groove (Line in the Sound, 2015)
Para la Raza (For the People) (Maniax, 2016)
Cruzando Borders (Smithsonian Folkways, 2018)**

*Grammy winner
**Grammy nominee

LOS TEXMANIACS

Max Baca (bajo sexto), Michael Guerra (accordion), Israel "Speedy" Villanueva (bass), Chente Barrera (drums). https://youtu.be/jj_I95WyiE4.
Library of Congress, September 11, 2013. https://youtu.be/yP1WSgyzWtA.
Millennium Stage, September 20, 2018. https://youtu.be/gb2MHDYnqbs.
California, December 6, 2018. (Set 1) https://youtu.be/cRDYt5VqoiE;
    (Set 2) https://youtu.be/bzuVMixcpHE.

FLACO JIMÉNEZ AND MAX BACA

Flaco Jiménez & Friends, Sycuan Casino, January 25, 2013. https://youtu.be
    /c60a_WAfWPA.
Flaco Jiménez y Su Conjunto, Tejano Conjunto Festival, San Antonio, 2013.
    https://youtu.be/ovWoumAQ2MQ.

THE TEXAS TORNADOS

Austin City Limits, 1999. https://youtu.be/ZT3U2jQ_SzE.

Bajo Sexto. Descended from a long line of seventeenth- and eighteenth-century chordophones, the twelve-string (six double-coursed) bajo sexto is believed to have originated in the state of Durango, Mexico. It was introduced to the United States at the end of the nineteenth century and joined with the accordion as the heart of Tex-Mex music.

Bolero (2/4 time in Cuba, 4/4 elsewhere). Not to be confused with the bolero popular in the ballrooms of Spain during the late eighteenth century, the "Cuban bolero" was developed by poetic, guitar-playing itinerant musicians (trovadores) a century later. The father of the Trova movement, Santiago de Cuba–born guitarist/songwriter Pepe Sánchez (1856–1918), is credited with creating the Cuban bolero.

Canción Ranchera. Originating before the Mexican Revolution (1846–1848) on ranches and in country villages, Canción Rancheras were sung by soloists accompanied by guitar. Lyrics were punctuated by enthusiastic yelling by the musician or audience.

Chicano Rock. Influenced by the Chicano Movement of the 1960s and pioneered by Tucson-born Eduardo "Lalo" Guerrero (1916–2005), this musical style combines English lyrics, Chicano slang, and R&B, country music, and rock arrangements.

Conjunto. A small musical group usually comprising accordion, bajo sexto, drums and bass.

Corrido. An up-tempo style of canción ranchera that conveys long epic tales about heroes, great deeds, and political/social issues. A popular subgenre, the narcocorrido, focuses on drug lords and cartels.

Cumbia (2/4 time). This music and dance style's name derives from the Equatorial Guinean word *cumbé,* meaning "dance." Traditionally played on flutes and other woodwinds, guitars, ouds, drums, and percussion instruments including maracas, it mixes African rhythms with Indigenous and European melodies, choreography, and dress. It originated during Colombia's days of slavery in the late 17th century and became popular throughout Latin America. Dancers move in a relaxed, "quick-quick-slow," circular-shaped movement. Less intricate than salsa, cumbia's basic steps may have originated because the slaves who originally danced it had their legs shackled. During the 1940s, multi-instrumentalist/composer Lucho Bermúdez (1912–1994) introduced Colombian Caribbean rhythms, including the cumbia, into contemporary music. In the 1950s, vocalist Luis Carlos Meyer Castandet (1916–1998) moved to Mexico and joined Rafael de Paz's Orquestra to record possibly the first cumbia record outside of Colombia.

Diatonic Accordion (melodeon). A free-reed squeeze box with one or more rows of buttons. Unlike the chromatic or piano accordion, a diatonic accordion produces different sounds when the bellows are pulled and pushed.

Guitarra Doble. A twelve-string pre–bajo sexto chordophone, related to the fourteen-string guitarra séptima and eight-string guitarra quinto, and first played in the Huasteca region along the Gulf of Mexico.

Huapango. A complex musical style and folk dance from the Huasteca region. It is sung in a strong, high-pitched voice, accompanied by a large-bodied eight-string guitarra quinta huapanguera, a five-string jarana huasteca, and violins.

Jig. A brisk, compound-meter folk dance with kicking and leaping movements, possibly taking its name from the Middle French *giguer* ("to dance" or "to jump"). Originating in northern England and Scotland in the sixteenth century, its popularity spread to Ireland by the eighteenth century. From there, it moved on to Eastern Europe, where it provided the final movement of the Baroque dance suite. Jigs were originally played in 12/8 time, but evolved into a variety of tempos, especially 6/8. The hop or slip jig is a step dance in 9/8 time. Jigs are improvised and danced with a rigid torso, the arms straight down, and quick footwork.

Mariachi. A traditional folk music that, legend has it, originated in the town of Cocula in the Mexican state of Jalisco in the nineteenth century. Initially a staple of Mexican weddings, mariachi requires at least two violins, two trumpets, a Spanish guitar, a high-pitched, five-stringed vihuela, and a guitarrón (acoustic bass). The mariachi son mixes Spanish, Indigenous, and African traditions.

Mazurka. (3/8 time with accent on the second or third beat) A highly improvisational triple-meter dance/music characterized by stamping feet and clicking heels. It originated in the sixteenth century in east central Poland as a four- or eight-couple dance.

Norteño Music. Traditionally played on accordion, bajo sexto, electric bass, drums, congas, and saxophone, and originating in northern Mexico, Norteño music features socially relevant lyrics and mostly polka and waltz rhythms.

Polka. Popular social/wedding dance, described by some as "the Viennese waltz adapted to 2/4 time." The polka's "quick-quick-slow" steps are sometimes attributed to Anna Slezakova (née Chadimova) of Labska Tynice, Bohemia, who called it "Mad ̌era" when she danced it during a folk song, "Strycek Nimra Koupil Simla" (Uncle Nimra Bought a White Horse), in 1834. Promoted by music teacher Josef Neruda, it became popular in the ballrooms of Prague within a year. The upper-class citizens of Vienna had adopted it by 1839, and it continued to Paris, where it sparked "polkamania," and London. It was introduced to the United States in 1844. The dance's name possibly derives from the Czech word *půlka*, meaning "half" or "half step." It evolved into the two-step, Zydeco (with a tap on the slow beat), Balboa (with a kick on the slow beat), shag, salsa, rumba, foxtrot, and more.

Redova or *redowa.* (3/4 time) A folk music/dance characterized by leaping steps, with couples doing a full rotation every sixth beat, and popular in Victorian-era ballrooms. Originating in Prague in 1829, it fell out of favor before being revived in Bohemia and London in 1846.

Schottische. A partnered, round dance variation of polka done in 4/4 or slow 2/4 time. Though an 1860 book credited Poland-born dancing master Markowski with creating it in his Paris studio in 1850, it was known in Bohemia as "the Rheinlander" at least six years before, and became popularly known as "the Bohemian polka." In 1850, a London dance teacher referred to it as "a German peasant dance." The name derives from the German word for "Scottish." Introduced to Mexico as the "chotis," it took on more rustic qualities. Variations in Texas include Drunk, Blue Bonnet, McGinty, and Douglas. The dance combines polka movements and a circular hop.

Tejano. A person of Mexican descent living in southern Texas.

Waila (Chicken Scratch). Instrumental dance music originating with the Tohono O'odham Nation in southern Arizona. A mixture of German, Spanish, and Norteño waila (polkas), chotes (schottisches), cumbias, and mazurkas are played on accordion, alto saxophone, guitar, bass, and drums. The dancers move counterclockwise.

CHAPTER ONE

1. Flaco tried making the enchiladas one time. "He called and asked for the recipe," my mother says. "I gave it to him, but in Texas, they don't have green chiles like they do in New Mexico. It doesn't come out the same."

CHAPTER TWO

1. Jim Washburn, "Flaco Jiménez . . . by Popular Demand," *Los Angeles Times*, July 19, 1994.

2. Washburn, "Flaco Jiménez . . . By Popular Demand."

3. Stephen Ide, "Peter Rowan: Bluegrass Boy," *Bluegrass Unlimited*, May 1997.

CHAPTER THREE

1. "Freddy Fender, 69, Legend in Texas and Country Music, Dies," *New York Times*, October 15, 2006.

CHAPTER SIX

1. "Texas Tornados—*4 Aces*," *No Depression*, September 1, 1996.

CHAPTER SEVEN

1. Spencer Leigh, "Obituary: Doug Sahm," *The Independent*, November 29, 1999.

2. Jack Hurst, "Wasted Days Are Over for Freddy Fender," *Chicago Tribune*, April 2, 1988.

3. "Demographic Profiles of Adult Offenders in Louisiana State Penitentiary," Louisiana Department of Public Safety and Corrections fact sheet, http://www.lajudi cialcollege.org/wp-content/uploads/2012/10/A-1.-LSP-Angola-Demographics-4-2012. pdf.

4. John Lear and E. W. Stagg, "America's Worst Prison," *Collier's*, Nov. 22, 1952: 13–16.

5. John Broven, *South to Louisiana: The Music of the Cajun Bayous* (Gretna, LA: Pelican, 1983), 281–82.

6. Joe Nick Patoski, "Sex, Drugs, and Rock and Roll," *Texas Monthly*, May 1996.

7. Patoski, "Sex, Drugs, and Rock and Roll."

8. "Huey Meaux and How He Brought Freddy Fender to Fame," compiled by Sarah Rolen, https://www.youtube.com/watch?v=uqfj_uVygUk.

9. "Huey Meaux."

10. Mario Tarradell, "Singer Freddy Fender Dies at Age 69," *Dallas Morning News*, October 15, 2006.

11. Leigh, "Obituary: Doug Sahm."

12. "100 Greatest Country Artists of All Time," *Rolling Stone*, June 15, 2017, https://www.rollingstone.com/music/music-lists/100-greatest-country-artists-of-all-time-195775/doug-sahm-203620.

13. Leigh, "Obituary: Doug Sahm."

14. "The Story of Outlaw Country in 33 Songs," *Pitchfork*, https://pitchfork.com/features/lists-and-guides/the-story-of-outlaw-country-in-33-songs.

15. Quoted in Leigh, "Obituary: Doug Sahm."

CHAPTER EIGHT

1. "Meet the Beatles for Real," Sept. 9, 2015, http://www.meetthebeatlesforreal.com/2015/09/chicken-skin-music.html.

CHAPTER ELEVEN

1. "Freddy Fender Has Incurable Cancer," Associated Press, August 3, 2006.

2. "Freddy Fender, 69, Legend in Texas and Country Music, Dies," *New York Times*, October 15, 2006.

Arrarás, Maria Celeste. 2015. *Selena's Secret: The Revealing Story behind Her Tragic Death*. New York: Atria.

Broyles-González, Yolanda. 2001. *Lydia Mendoza's Life in Music/La Historia de Lydia Mendoza: Norteño Tejano Legacies*. New York: Oxford University Press.

Burr, Ramiro. 1999. *Billboard Guide to Tejano and Regional Mexican Music*. New York: Billboard.

Clark, Walter Aaron. 2002. *From Tejano to Tango: Latin American Popular Music*. New York: Routledge.

De León, Arnoldo, ed. 2012. *War along the Border: The Mexican Revolution and Tejano Communities*. College Station: Texas A&M University Press.

———. 2015. *Tejano West Texas*. College Station: Texas A&M University Press.

Dyer, John, and Juan Tejeda. 2005. *Conjunto: Voz del Pueblo, Canciones del Corazón*. Austin: University of Texas Press.

Hartman, Gary. 2008. *The History of Texas Music*. College Station: Texas A&M University Press.

Joseph, Harriett Denise. 2018. *From Santa Anna to Selena: Notable Mexicanos and Tejanos in Texas History since 1821*. Denton: University of North Texas Press.

Munson, Sammye. 1989. *Our Tejano Heroes: Outstanding Mexican-Americans in Texas*. Austin: Eakin Press.

Nunez, Soledad Adelita. 2015. "Sin las Mujeres No Hay Conjunto: Mapping Chicana Feminisms in the Performances of Susan Torres, Clemencia Zapata, and Ruby Franco." Masters thesis, University of Texas at San Antonio.

Paredes, Américo. 1995. *A Texas-Mexican Cancionero: Folksongs of the Lower Border*. Austin: University of Texas Press.

Patoski, Joe Nick. 1997. *Selena: Como la Flor*. New York: Berkley.

Pedelty, Mark. 2010. *Musical Ritual in Mexico City: From the Aztec to NAFTA*. Austin: University of Texas Press.

Peña, Manuel H. 1985. *The Texas-Mexican Conjunto: History of a Working-Class Music*. Austin: University of Texas Press.

———. 1999. *Música Tejana: The Cultural Economy of Artistic Transformation*. College Station: Texas A&M University Press.

Perez, Chris. 2013. *To Selena, with Love*. New York: Celebra.

Ragland, Catherine. 2009. *Música Norteña: Mexican Migrants Creating a Nation between Nations*. Philadelphia: Temple University Press.

San Miguel, Guadalupe, Jr. 2002. *Tejano Proud: Tex-Mex Music in the Twentieth Century*. College Station: Texas A&M University Press.

Stimeling, Travis D. 2011. *Cosmic Cowboys and New Hicks: The Countercultural Sounds of Austin's Progressive Country Music Scene*. New York: Oxford University Press.

Tejeda, Juan, and Avelardo Valdez, eds. 2001. *Puro Conjunto: An Album in Words and Pictures: Writings, Posters, and Photographs from the Tejano Conjunto Festival en San Antonio, 1982–1998*. Austin: CMAS Books.

Valdez, Carlos. 2006. *Justice for Selena: The State vs Yolanda Saldivar*. Victoria, BC: Trafford.

Vargas, Deborah R. 2012. *Dissonant Divas in Chicana Music: The Limits of la Onda*. Minneapolis: University of Minnesota Press.

Villarreal, Mary Ann. 2017. *Listening to Rosita: The Business of Tejana Music and Culture, 1930–1955*. Norman: University of Oklahoma Press.

Wald, Elijah. 2002. *Narcocorrido: A Journey into the Music of Drugs, Guns, and Guerrillas*. New York: Rayo.

? & the Mysterians, 118

4 Aces, 56, 59, 60, 61, 90, 178, 185

About Time, 130, 179
accordion, 3, 4, 10, 16, 18, 1, 2, 3, 4, 5, 6, 7, 12,
    14, 17, 18, 19, 20, 22, 23, 24, 25, 26, 30, 34,
    36, 38, 39, 40, 41, 48, 50, 51, 52, 60, 61, 69,
    73, 82, 83, 93, 96, 98, 101, 103, 106, 109, 112,
    116, 123, 124, 125, 126, 128, 129, 130, 131, 133,
    134, 139, 140, 141, 145, 147, 149, 150, 172, 173,
    180, 181, 182, 183, 184
"Across the Borderline," 84
"Alligator Alley," 173
Almeida, Santiago, 10, 3, 4
Americano Groove, 144, 145, 146, 179
"Amor de Mi Vida (Love of My Life)," 144
Anderson, Pete, 19, 105
Antone, Clifford, 56, 83, 85, 86, 87, 91
A Prairie Home Companion, 133, 145
Arhoolie, 20
Arista, 18, 93, 102, 178
Asleep at the Wheel, 8, 18, 56, 138, 149
Austin, 8, 18, 19, 23, 34, 44, 45, 56, 60, 64, 72,
    73, 74, 78, 86, 88, 89, 90, 103, 105, 106, 109,
    111, 113, 115, 124, 137, 150, 178, 180, 188, 189
Austin City Limits, 18, 19, 23, 73, 180
"Ay Te Dejo en San Antonio," 19, 138
The Aztecs, 106

Baca, Baltazar, 5
Baca, Carlos, 6, 8, 12, 44, 63, 136, 163, 164, 165,
    166, 176, 182, 189
Baca, Gloria, 7, 12
Baca, Jimmy, 8, 12, 17, 5, 6, 7, 12, 15, 17, 18, 23,
    24, 25, 26, 38, 40, 41, 42, 46, 47, 49, 50, 51,
    54, 55, 89, 90, 147, 148, 176
Baca, Josh, 8, 12, 16, 17, 18, 26, 33, 34, 50, 51, 52,
    89, 90, 101, 108, 109, 126, 135, 138, 139, 140,
    144, 145, 147, 148, 149, 150, 151, 152, 158, 160,
    161, 167, 169, 172, 173, 174, 176
Baca, Max, 3, 7, 8, 9, 10, 11, 12, 13, 14, 15, 16, 17,
    18, 19, 3, 4, 5, 12, 14, 15, 17, 20, 25, 26, 28, 30,
    35, 37, 44, 45, 47, 48, 49, 51, 53, 56, 58, 61, 73,
    80, 81, 89, 95, 97, 98, 100, 101, 102, 105, 106,
    108, 109, 111, 112, 126, 127, 129, 130, 132, 134,
    135, 136, 138, 141, 142, 143, 145, 147, 148, 149,
    150, 151, 153, 161, 164, 165, 166, 167, 169, 171,
    173, 174, 176, 178, 180
Baca, Max Don, Sr., 1, 5, 6, 7
Baca, Maxine, 8, 5, 7, 50, 90
Baca, Mya Jole, 165
bajo sexto, 3, 4, 7, 8, 10, 12, 15, 17, 19, 1, 3, 4, 14,
    17, 20, 21, 22, 24, 25, 26, 27, 28, 30, 33, 36,
    40, 45, 46, 48, 51, 53, 54, 56, 57, 58, 60, 61,
    73, 76, 83, 89, 90, 92, 98, 99, 101, 102, 103,
    105, 109, 114, 116, 125, 127, 129, 130, 134, 135,
    137, 138, 139, 142, 145, 146, 147, 150, 151, 166,
    169, 172, 173, 180, 181, 182, 183

Banda Brava, 96

bandolón, 12

Barber, Jack, 69, 75, 82, 85

The Beatles, 2, 32, 75, 83, 105, 141, 142, 187

Beatty, Leon, 75

"Before the Next Teardrop Falls," 70

Benson, Ray

Berlin, Steve, 12, 18, 106, 111, 112, 118, 119, 126, 141, 145, 146, 176

Bernal, Eloy, 4

Berry, Chuck, 28, 86, 95

Beyoncé, 136

Bill Boyd & His Cowboy Ramblers, 12

Bill Monroe & the Bluegrass Boys, 28

Blank, Les, 19

boleros, 133

Borders y Bailes, 17, 132, 134, 138, 151, 175, 179

Bromberg, David, 82

Buena Suerte, 18, 105, 178

Cadena, Roberto, 21

Campisi, Tony, 34

"Canción Mixteca," 134

Carter, President Jimmy, 85

Chicken Skin Music, 83

Clapton, Eric, 15, 32, 33

Clements, Vassar, 27

Conjunto, 16, 17, 19, 1, 18, 20, 22, 40, 48, 101, 116, 121, 122, 131, 138, 141, 175, 180, 181, 188

Conjunto Aztlan, 16, 48

Conjunto Festival, 16, 19, 48, 101, 116, 131, 180, 188

Cooder, Ry, 18, 27, 31, 33, 57, 61, 62, 83, 134

Creedence Clearwater Revival, 32, 52, 84, 173

Cruzando Borders, 17, 84, 107, 149, 151, 179

cumbias, 28, 118, 128, 133, 184

Danny Ezba & the Goldens, 75

De La Rosa,Tony, 17, 49, 126, 142

The Dell Kings, 65

Díaz, Eduardo, 16, 1, 48, 176

D.L.B. Records, 22

Domenici, PIetro, 36

Douglas, Jerry, 6, 29, 30, 33, 63, 75, 76, 172, 183

"Down in the Barrio," 144

Downs, LIla, 134

Dr. John, 82

Durawa, Ernie, 9, 74, 94

Dylan, Bob, 18, 82, 83, 87

The Eagles, 142

Earle, Steve, 29, 78

Earth Opera, 29

Eddie Dugosh & the Ah-Ha Playboys, 65

Edwards, Don, 29

El Conjunto Bernal, 4, 121

El Fronterizo, 24

Elida y Avante, 140, 142

"El Pantalon Blue Jean," 22

Ely, Joe, 18, 106, 111, 112, 144, 150

Escobar, Alejandro, 144

Escoveda, Alejandro, 18

Farías, David, 12, 126, 127, 128, 132, 135, 138, 139, 144, 148, 149, 153, 176

Fender, Freddy, 6, 8, 18, 9, 10, 35, 53, 54, 57, 58, 59, 60, 61, 66, 67, 68, 70, 71, 72, 73, 74, 78, 84, 87, 91, 92, 94, 105, 106, 111, 112, 117, 118, 120, 140, 185, 186, 187

Fierro, Martin, 82

Fitch, Charles, 65, 66

Flores, Bobby, 18, 106

Fogerty, John, 32

Fowler, Kevin, 18, 145

The Free Mexican Airforce, 27, 28, 29, 31, 169

Fuentes, Rick, 8, 18

Gabriel, Juan, 41

Garcia, Isaac, 57

Garcia, Jerry, 27

Garcia, Óscar, 130, 135, 142

Garrett, Amos, 86

Garza, Mike, 21

Glenn Miller, 12

Goldberg, Barry, 84

Graceland, 119

Granata, Rocco, 133

Greene, Richard, 29

Green Grass Gringos, 27

Grisman, David, 27, 29

Groover's Paradise, 84
Guerra, Michael, 123, 126, 180
Guerrero, Eduardo "Lalo," 100, 149, 181
guitarra séptima, 12, 182
Guzman, Joel, 8, 106, 123, 150

Hangin' on by a Thread, 59
Harris, Emmylou, 18
Harrison, George, 83, 87
Hernandez, Jesse, 128
Hernandez, Little Joe, 19, 109, 137
Hernandez, Noel, 12, 15, 17, 18, 14, 51, 58, 135, 140, 148
Herrera, Roger, 21
"Hey Baby (Qué Pasó?)," 38, 79, 87
Hiatt, John, 84
Hidalgo, David
Hillbilly Lounge, 28
Hohner Instrument Company, 8, 1, 2, 19
The Honkey Blues Band, 77
"How Can a Beautiful Woman Be So Ugly," 145

International Accordion Festival, 49
"I Wanna Know Your Name," 144

Jagger, Mick, 98
jarana jarocha, 12
Jasper, Pat, 49
Jay, Little Jimmy, 65
Jiménez, Don Santiago, 138
Jiménez, Leonardo "Flaco," 6, 7, 8, 10, 12, 15, 16, 18, 19, 3, 17, 18, 19, 20, 21, 22, 23, 24, 25, 26, 27, 28, 30, 31, 32, 33, 35, 41, 46, 47, 48, 49, 51, 52, 53, 54, 57, 58, 59, 60, 61, 64, 72, 73, 82, 83, 84, 86, 87, 91, 92, 93, 94, 95, 96, 97, 98, 99, 100, 101, 102, 103, 104, 105, 106, 108, 109, 112, 113, 114, 116, 120, 121, 124, 125, 126, 131, 133, 136, 138, 139, 140, 141, 142, 147, 148, 149, 159, 163, 165, 167, 168, 169, 171, 172, 176, 178, 180, 185
Jiménez, Patrico, 19
Jiménez, Don Santiago, Sr., 19, 20, 21
Joey Records, 22, 47
John, Elton, 83
The Johnny Canales Show, 48

Johnson, Jimmy, 65
Jordan, Esteban, 18, 49, 101, 102, 124, 157
"Just Enough Rope (Bastante Cordón)," 110

Keith, Bill, 28, 29
King, Riley "B. B.," 32, 33
The Kinks, 77
Kirchen, Bill, 33
The Knights, 65
Kristofferson, Kris, 78, 80
The Kumbia Kings, 122

"La Bamba," 37, 52, 118, 119, 125
Lady Gaga, 136
La Música de Baldemar Huerta, 71
"Land of the Navajo," 27
La Tropa F, 128
Laws, William James "Willie J.," 130, 146
Legends and Legacies, 19, 147, 178
"A Little Is Better than Nada," 61
Live from the Limo, 56, 91, 133, 178
Live in Bremen, 86
Live in Japan, 86
Logan, Tex, 27
Longoria, Valerio, 4, 17, 126
Longoria, Valero, 4
López, Trini, 118
Los Alegres de Terán, 149
Los Caminantes, 21
Los Cenzontles, 149
Los Compadres Farías, 128
Los Frijoles Románticos, 142, 151
Los Hermanos Baca, 17, 41, 46, 47, 90, 120, 125, 149
Los Lobos, 8, 12, 18, 19, 33, 76, 105, 106, 118, 125, 140, 141, 145, 150
Los Lobos, Los Super Seven, 18, 33, 106, 111, 125, 126, 145
Los Super Seven, 18, 105, 106, 108, 110, 112, 126, 150, 178
Los Texmaniacs, 6, 8, 9, 11, 12, 14, 15, 16, 17, 18, 19, 28, 39, 65, 76, 84, 107, 108, 123, 124, 126, 129, 130, 131, 132, 134, 135, 138, 139, 140, 142, 143, 144, 145, 147, 148, 162, 166, 167, 169, 171, 175

Los Tuscanes de Tijuana, 133
Louisiana State Penitentiary, 67
Lovett, Lyle, 18, 148, 150
Lucero, Millie, 8

Macias, Martin, 3, 26, 27, 33, 99
Mahal, Taj, 33, 81
"Marina," 47, 133
The Markays, 65
Martínez, Lorenzo, 10, 12, 17, 18, 4, 26, 96, 100,
    122, 125, 126, 135, 142, 145, 146, 153, 162, 176
Martínez, Narciso, 10, 2, 3, 4, 6, 17, 21, 141,
    142, 146
Mavericks, 18, 86, 101, 112, 123, 146
McClinton, Delbert, 33
Meaux, Huey Purvis, 68, 69, 70, 71, 75, 85, 186
Meaux, Stanislaus, 69
"Mendocino," 78
Meyers, Augie, 6, 8, 12, 18, 22, 38, 53, 54, 57,
    59, 60, 61, 71, 72, 73, 74, 75, 76, 77, 78, 82,
    85, 86, 87, 91, 92, 94, 106, 111, 112, 113, 140,
    145, 176
Michael Martin Murphey's Wild West Fest, 92
Midnight Sun, 86
Mi Primer Amor, 38, 178
Montez, Chris, 118
Morales, Rocky, 64, 75, 82, 87, 105
Morante, Jose, 22
"A Mover el Bote," 133
Muleskinner, 29
The Mysterious Sam Dogg and the Cosmic
    Cowboys, 92

Nelson, Willie, 16, 45, 55, 56, 60, 65, 67, 75, 78,
    95, 130, 141, 142
The Newbeats, 77
"Nuevo Laredo," 78

O'Connor, Mark, 30
Owens, Buck, 18, 105
Owens. Charlie, 82

Para la Raza, 147
Parnell, Lee Roy, 104
Perez, Johnny, 64, 75

The Pharaohs, 65
polka, 3, 4, 7, 12, 14, 15, 17, 19, 21, 22, 32, 38, 39,
    51, 64, 76, 123, 133, 141, 145, 146, 158, 183, 184
Ponce, Jesse, 24, 26, 30, 169
Pulido, Roberto, 121, 148

Ramos, Ruben, 8, 18, 19, 106, 109, 124, 125, 137
Randolph, Robert, 33, 34
redovas, 1, 133, 141
Reiniger, Pete, 133, 135
The Return of the Formerly Brothers, 86
Reyes, Gilbert, 8, 1, 2, 72, 122, 176
Rice, Tony, 29, 172
Richards, Keith, 98, 99
The Righteous Brothers, 77
Rio Records, 21
Rocky & the Border Kings, 78
Rodríguez, Robert, 115
Rodríguez, Roberto, 40
The Rolling Stones, 18, 36, 75, 77, 86, 97, 98,
    100, 121, 138, 178
Ronstadt, Linda, 18, 117
Rooney, Jim, 28
Rosas, Cesar, 18, 33, 76, 105, 106, 125, 126
Rowan, Peter, 12, 18, 27, 28, 29, 30, 31, 32, 51, 57,
    83, 125, 143, 167, 169, 170, 172, 173, 176, 185
Ruben's Place, 124
"Running Out of Reasons to Run," 110

Sahm, Doug "Sir Douglas," 8, 18, 9, 10, 18, 22,
    53, 54, 55, 56, 58, 59, 60, 61, 62, 63, 64, 65,
    66, 71, 72, 73, 74, 75, 76, 77, 78, 79, 82, 83,
    84, 85, 86, 87, 88, 91, 92, 94, 105, 106, 112,
    113, 124, 140, 186
Sahm, Shawn, 75, 92, 112, 113
Said and Done, 18, 105, 112, 178
Saint Therese Catholic School, 36
Saldaña, 64, 78
Saldivar, Mingo, 8, 19, 58, 101, 121, 124, 126, 189
Sam the Sham and the Pharoahs, 118
San Antonio, 10, 15, 17, 19, 3, 16, 18, 19, 20, 21,
    22, 25, 27, 30, 47, 48, 54, 63, 64, 65, 66, 71,
    72, 74, 77, 81, 82, 90, 99, 102, 105, 118, 120,
    124, 130, 135, 138, 139, 149, 157, 159, 162, 166,
    175, 180, 188, 189

Santana, Carlos, 15, 32, 33, 95, 118, 137
Santiago Jiménez y Sus Valedores, 21
Savoy, Marc, 173
Sawtelle, Charles, 146
schottisches, 1, 3, 4, 133, 141, 184
Seatrain, 29
Selena, 6, 120, 121, 122, 187, 188, 189
Señorita, 18, 105, 178
"She Can't Say I Didn't Cry," 110
Sheehy, David, 6, 8, 11, 12, 19, 132, 134, 136, 150, 176
Shocked. Michelle, 146
The Sir Douglas Quintet, 64, 75, 76, 77, 78, 82, 86, 92, 125
Sleepytown, 18, 105, 178
Slim, Guitar (Eddie Jones), 85
Smithsonian Folkways, 8, 11, 17, 19, 132, 136, 147, 149, 167, 178, 179
Smithsonian Latino Center, 16, 1
Sonet Records, 22
Sparks, Speedy, 9, 86
Squeeze Box King, 19, 178
Stanton, Harry Dean, 134
Statman, Andy, 82
Stills, Stephen, 18
Strachwitz, Chris. See Arhoolie
The Streets of Bakersfield, 18, 19

Taylor, Gene, 86
Tejano, 12, 16, 17, 19, 18, 20, 23, 31, 39, 48, 62, 64, 90, 97, 101, 102, 105, 110, 112, 116, 118, 120, 121, 122, 123, 127, 129, 130, 131, 132, 135, 141, 142, 146, 148, 151, 166, 175, 180, 183, 187, 188
Tejeda, Juan, 8, 16, 4, 48, 49, 131, 176, 188
Tellez, Óscar, 8, 9, 10, 26, 33, 35, 53, 57, 58, 59, 92, 101, 103, 105, 113, 114, 115, 116, 138, 142, 147, 165
Texas Rock for Country Rollers, 85
The Texas Tornados, 8, 10, 11, 18, 9, 10, 18, 19, 32, 33, 52, 53, 54, 55, 56, 57, 59, 61, 67, 71, 72, 73, 79, 85, 87, 88, 90, 91, 92, 94, 96, 102, 105, 111, 112, 113, 120, 121, 123, 124, 126, 133, 140, 163, 164, 185

Texas Towns & Tex-Mex Sounds, 17, 19, 65, 179
Tex-Mex, conjunto, Tejano, 4, 12, 15, 16, 17, 18, 19, 2, 3, 19, 22, 23, 28, 31, 32, 36, 46, 64, 65, 76, 79, 84, 87, 96, 97, 98, 125, 138, 140, 147, 173, 174, 179, 181, 188
Tin Cup, 11
Together after Five, 78
Traveling Wilburys, 87
Treviño, Joe, 8, 12, 19, 84, 102, 135, 177
Trevino, Rick, 8, 12, 18, 52, 105, 107, 109, 111, 124, 145, 151, 177

Uncle Tupelo, 85

Val, Joe, 28
Valens, Ritchie, 52, 117, 118, 119
Valle, Ruben, 40, 57
Vamos Albuquerque! (Let's Go Albuquerque), 7
Vaughn, Stevie Ray, 32, 56
Vavages, Stevie Ray, 166
Veerkamp, Frederick, 1, 2
Verhyden, Dwayne, 19
Villanueva, Israel "Speedy," 123, 125, 180
Villareal, Bruno, 40
"Viva Seguín," 24
Voodoo Lounge, 18, 97, 178

Was, Don, 97, 98
"Wasted Days and Wasted Nights," 67, 70, 71, 78, 120
The Western Head Music Co., 38
White, Clarence, 29, 75, 79, 183
Who Are These Masked Men?, 86
Williams, Hank, 16, 64, 141, 142

Ybarra, Pete, 123
Yoakam, Dwight, 18, 23, 105

Zimmerle, Fred, 19
Zimmerle, Henry, 21
Zone of Our Own, 59